Whispers in the Dark:
True Ghost Stories and Eerie Tales

by

Cyn Shrader Hill

Copyright © 2018 Cyn Shrader Hill
All rights reserved.
ISBN-13: 978-1726640954
ISBN-10: 1726640957

DEDICATION

This book is dedicated to my Mom, the strongest woman I know and the best cheerleader a girl could ever hope to have.

Thank you for always believing in me when I don't, always raising my spirits up when I'm down, and inspiring me when I'm stuck.

Thank you for telling me stories of Uncle Ira and the rest of the family. I've enjoyed hour upon hour of tales about everyone, and I could sit for hours more talking with you. I appreciate you always listening to my stories even in rough draft form plus giving me the needed feedback for each one. I am forever grateful for your unconditional love and generosity, and I'm blessed to call you "Mom."

I love you more than you'll ever know and more than I can ever say in words. You've helped me through some of my scariest and lowest times - always a beacon in the darkness. I thank God for you every day.

You are a remarkable lady, and if I'm lucky enough to become half the woman you are, then I'll be undeniably blessed.

ACKNOWLEDGMENTS

Thank you, Lord, for all that You are and thank you for blessing me with words when I need them.

My Husband Gregg, who enabled me to chase my dreams. Thank you for letting me branch out into writing and giving me help in different areas, even the paranormal world when you really didn't want me to go there. I love you, Handsome Man.

R.W. Groom, my favorite English teacher, who taught me to love writing stories way back when. Thank you for granting me the privilege of telling *The Music Lesson*.

Mark Elliott Fults, my genuinely extraordinary friend who has taught me so many things about the paranormal, strange occurrences, and life in general. I can't thank you enough for calming me down many nights when something stressful was happening. You never cease to amaze me with your gifts, talents, and generosity. Thank you for the beautiful cover art and stunning illustrations you have done for me, as well as the EVP team design. Thank you for trusting me to edit your books, for giving me the nudge I needed to start writing and thank you for introducing me to Teal. I love you very much, My Dear Friend.

Teal L. Gray, who welcomed me into her world of writing, editing and publishing without a backward glance. You are a breath of fresh air! Thank you for believing in me and for allowing me to be a part of your many projects. Your words of encouragement and inspiration have helped me more than you know. I am blessed to have you in my life. Love you!

Sean Rader, my EVP Co-founder who has been there in the dark and in brighter times. Thank you for telling your stories and for sharing time with me during our many investigations. I appreciate your phone calls, texts, and messages more than you realize. You are irreplaceable and very much loved.

Matthew Yeager, my friend the ghost magnet that can sniff out a specter faster than any sensitive I know. Thank you for always being there and for sharing your stories with me. You are very much appreciated and loved.

Lawrence "Yoda" Bailey, my old college friend and EVP teammate who has helped me with many investigations. Thank you for helping me finish *Time Warp*. Your time is appreciated. Love you, my friend.

Chrissy Wolfe Rumford, my amazing friend who keeps me laughing and always builds up my self-esteem. There's not another one like you in this entire world. You are a force to be reckoned with! Love you!

Valerie Tallent Young and her wonderful family including Buck and her sweet mom, Sandra, my sweet friend and her family who have invited me into their lives and shared some tremendous stories with me. Also, thank you for allowing me to be your Storyteller for special events :)

A Special Shout Out to those that have had their names changed to protect their privacy: Ernest and Anna; Amy, Georgia Ann, Riley, Lloyd, Chuck, and Doug; Emily, Briley, Lydia, and Howie; Melinda and Karl; Justine and Donatien. You know who you are :) Thank you for telling or allowing me to tell your amazing stories. I appreciate you all and hope I've brought at least a bit of sunshine into your days.

FOREWARD

By Teal Gray Rev., N.D.

Rarely does a new author come along with a seasoned author's command of storytelling like Cyn Shrader Hill. I have no doubt you will join me in being captivated by the twenty-three true tales included in this book.

I have worked with Cyn on several projects. In my over thirty years in the paranormal field as an experiencer, researcher and writer, what impressed me most besides her writing skill is her genuine interest and curiosity in uncovering what lies beyond the veil she has been gifted to peek through.

Cyn takes you on a journey that respects and tries to understand these spirits and entities. I love that she never forgets she is dealing with once flesh and blood souls like you and I trying to make a connection from beyond the grave as they did in life.

TABLE OF CONTENTS

- My Bedtime Story
- Listen to Your Mother
- Premonitions
- The Music Lesson
- Through a Nightmare
- Step Inside Horns Creek
- The Mind is a Terrible Thing
- Reaching Through
- Abandoned House
- A Lady's Chifferobe
- The Gravel Road
- Tainted Land
- Drop Zone
- Uninvited
- Attachments
- Lynchburg Haunted Home
- Paranormal Email
- Redheaded Ghost
- Time Warp
- Intruder
- Problems at Home
- The Holiday Rush
- Stranger and Stranger

MY BEDTIME STORY

I've always enjoyed horror movies and scary stories. When I was a very young girl, I'd often beg my grandmother to tell me a particular story before bed about my great great uncle. Every night she'd argue, but after several pleas, she would entertain me because she knew I'd keep her awake until I heard it again. She told the tale as she was reciting a monologue of terror and would end with the words "BOO! Got you!" I'd happily giggle then she'd say "now, go to sleep." Here is my favorite bedtime story:

Late one night, Uncle Ira was riding horseback on his way home in the country when he was caught in a sudden very strong thunderstorm. He was soon drenched, flinching each time the lightning flashed, and the thunder roared and cracked. Luckily, he came upon a little church called *Prosperity*, and he quickly decided to take refuge inside. Hurriedly he tied his horse out of the weather beneath the overhang and ducked inside the unlocked church building. Relieved to be out of the raging storm, he walked through the dark sanctuary and sat down on one of the wooden pews.

He listened to the heavy rain hitting the roof and looked around the little church as the storm's lightning frequently lit up the room. Though he'd much rather be at home, he started to relax. The storm raged, and the rain beat down harder, but Uncle Ira stretched his legs out and decided to close his eyes.

Somewhere in the darkness came a sound: *tip tap...rustle*. Uncle Ira's eyes flew open as his breath caught. What was that? The wind? A mouse? Maybe the horse just outside the door. Probably nothing. Shaking it off, he shook his head, smiling at his sudden startle. He was just paranoid. Taking a deep breath, he tried to relax again.

Tip tap.

Eyes wide in the darkness with his heart racing he thought "were those sounds footsteps?" Something was making a strange noise, and it was somewhere between his pew and the door behind him.

Tip tap...rustle.

He couldn't breathe. What was it? Now, there was only silence inside the church as the storm raged on. He turned slowly in his seat waiting for another lightning bolt to brighten the sanctuary. When it did, the crash of thunder was immediate, and Uncle Ira jumped, but he could see nothing odd or out of the ordinary anywhere inside the little country building. Turning to face front again he listened to the storm and tried to ignore his fear, but his ears were straining to hear the slightest sound, and so he waited.

Tip tap.

Surely, he was imagining this sound, or at the very least, making it something ominous when it was nothing. He told himself to relax.

Tip tap.

He refused to turn around again.

Tip tap...rustle.

His heart was pounding with fear, and his eyes could be no wider.

Tip tap.

If only he had gotten all the way home before the storm.

Tip tap.

Terror crept up his spine, and he could not ignore the sound. He waited in dread for the unknown to appear, white knuckles gripping the edge of his seat.

Tip tap. Closer and closer it came in the darkness toward him. *Tip tap... rustle. Tip tap.*

As the lightning flashed making the room unnaturally bright, he began to turn and look back one more time. Bony arms suddenly reached out grabbing him tightly. Uncle Ira screamed, jumping up, he broke away from those arms turning to look into the crazed eyes of a madwoman - hair disheveled, eyes wild and long fingers reaching out to grab him again.

It seems a resident had escaped from a local property known around the county as *The Poor House* that provided refuge for the downtrodden. Inhabitants of the home had nowhere else to go and were not claimed by anyone else - no one wanted them. There was a wide variety of tenants: widows and their children who had lost the breadwinner of their family, handicapped and mentally ill persons, and the very poorest of society. This particular woman, completely insane, found her way inside the dark church just as Uncle Ira did in the middle of a terrible storm. A church, usually a safe haven, had become a house of terror late that night for a country gentleman traveling alone headed home. It was an incident Uncle Ira never forgot, and a story his great-great-grandniece would beg to hear over and over for years to come.

LISTEN TO YOUR MOTHER

When EVP's Co-founder Sean was twelve, he spent the night with his two best friends, brothers, Daniel and David, at their house. They decided to play with the Ouija board to see if they could get it to "talk." After about thirty minutes of little to no activity, Sheila, the two boys' mother, caught them asking the board questions and was extremely upset. She snatched up the Ouija and threw it out into the yard yelling "I've told you not to play with that thing!" Afterward, she went to bed allowing the boys to stay up playing video games. Her husband Skip was working third shift.

Later, the three boys were playing on the Atari when they each thought they saw something walk down the hallway. Almost instantly, they heard Sheila scream. They all thought she was "messing with them" and trying to scare them because she'd told them not to play with the Ouija before. They cautiously walked down the hallway expecting her to throw open the door shouting "BOO!" The screams only became louder, and still half-way thinking she was pranking them, they smiled at each other and then went to open the door. The knob wouldn't budge. As each one of the boys tried to turn the doorknob and failed, they began to feel something may be wrong. The screaming continued.

Finally, after several minutes, Sheila opened the door and yelled at all three boys "I told you not to mess with that damn board!" She told them something had held her down on the bed, and she couldn't get away. The boys were still unconvinced but couldn't figure out why she was making such a big deal out of nothing. Afterall, nothing had happened while they'd played with the Ouija. They had tried for about thirty minutes without much luck to get the planchette to answer whatever questions they could think of to ask.

The next morning Skip came home, and Sheila told him about something pinning her to the bed after the three boys played with the Ouija board. She explained that something was standing over her staring down at her, and described the figure watching her like a coach spotting a weight-lifter who's about to bench press.

Rolling up her sleeves, she showed them all the bruises, complete handprints, on both of her upper arms near her shoulders. The marks displayed showed the thumb of each print on the inside of Sheila's upper arm, and the fingerprints splayed out pointing down toward her elbow. Each upper extremity showed imprints of four fingers and a thumb; a right-hand impression was displayed on her right-side upper biceps and a left-hand mark on her left arm. She couldn't have done that herself. It wasn't humanly possible.

Now the three boys knew she hadn't been joking around trying to scare them. But suddenly, they were even more scared; they knew Skip would punish them. Sean doesn't remember exactly what the punishment was but says Skip had spanked them for much less. He also feels pretty sure they were right to be scared of Skip's punishment.

Sean ended the story by telling me they burned the board and buried it in the backyard. To this day, after seeing the bruises on Sheila and hearing her bloodcurdling screams, he refuses to use a Ouija or any other talking board.

PREMONITIONS

My friend Valerie, an empath, has been a sensitive and open to the paranormal all of her life. I listened to many stories of strange sightings and unusual happenings that have occurred around her over the years. When she was a child, her family, the Tallents, bought a house from another family. The man in told them he felt like he needed to move because he thought his wife was going crazy; his wife told them she thought she was going insane because she kept seeing her son outside working his horse. That was impossible since their son had passed away at least three years before the property sold.

The woman had told the new owners a little history of the area. On the property was 'the big house' as they referred to the main home, and in the rear, a building that had been used as servants' quarters many years ago. Back then, a slave husband and wife had worked in the big house and the barn, and their two children, an eleven-year-old boy, and an eight-year-old girl had played for hours in the servants' area. Sadly, while the parents worked one day, the servants' quarters caught on fire and burned down taking the lives of their two children with it.

Valerie's family moved onto the property in the December of the year she turned eight years old, and her brother, Ricky, was eleven - the same ages of the children who had died years before in the fire. It seems her mother Sandra has a premonition or a type of strange sighting when something terrible is about to happen. About a week before school closed for the summer, Sandra looked up and saw her daughter's shadow moving back and forth. She told Val to go to bed except her daughter was already in bed asleep. Valerie was finishing third grade at the time. The day before school dismissed, Valerie broke her arm and remembered having to wear a cast almost all summer between third and fourth grade.

Later on, her mother saw Valerie's brother walking down the hall, and she started calling to him, but he never responded. She went out the back door looking for him and found him in the back pasture working on the fence. A few days later, while feeding the goat, it became enraged and started head-butting Ricky trying to kill him. Sandra happened to look out the back door, seeing what was happening and jumped over the deck railing yelling at her husband for help. A shotgun was brought to Mr. Tallent, and he shot the goat in the head, but the animal actually bleated at him and wouldn't stop. A second shot had to be fired, this one into the heart, to drop the goat.

Valerie has experienced similar things too, often getting strong warnings of danger, or *seeing* events before they happen. Valerie and Buck had been married only six months when she received a scary premonition - a plane exploding after takeoff. Buck, a Specialist in the Army Reserves, was being sent to the Panama Canal for two weeks and Valerie begged him not to go. She was afraid the plane taking him there would explode, but he told her he didn't think his Sergeant would cancel his trip just "because my wife saw something." For the next several days, she had the impression that she was about to become a newlywed widow. The day before Buck's departure, Valerie took the entire day off to spend with him since she thought that was going to be their last day together. That morning, they were watching the news on television while breakfast was being prepared. They watched as the Space Shuttle took off and as it went into the air, Valerie suddenly turned her head screaming. Buck asked her what was wrong, but she told him to "just watch, just watch." At that second, the craft blew up. She told him "that's the exact thing I saw," but she hadn't known it was the shuttle. Although she was mourning the country's loss, she knew the airplane transporting Buck would be fine.

Valerie has even experienced different scents waft through the air from no apparent source. One day as she was dressing for work, she could smell her brother Ricky's cologne even though he was not there. She called him at work, but another shop employee, David, told her that he was on delivery. While they were talking, another call was coming through on the second line to the shop from one of the workers. David told Valerie hurriedly "I've got to go! Ricky's truck just burst into flames! Thank Goodness they had just gotten out of it to deliver a couch!"

Valerie has also *seen* one of her uncles on her father's side of the family, Uncle Randy, standing out in a pasture with a glowing abdomen. She immediately called her aunt asking how he was feeling; Aunt Marie explained, "he's on the couch really sick. The doctor gave him antibiotics, but they don't really know what's going on." Valerie said, "I see glowing." to which her aunt questioned "what?" Valerie begged, "Just tell him I see glowing." Back at the doctor the next day, her uncle had to have a triple procedure performed immediately. The doctor told them then that they "caught it just in time."

On another occasion, after she and Buck had gotten home from work, Valerie smelled an overbearing odor of wine in her home. A friend was visiting at the time, but the only person that could detect the wine was Valerie. She looked at the three bottles of homemade wine a friend had given her, but the bottles weren't broken, so the smell wasn't coming from them. She called her mother and told her about the weird scent. Sandra came right over to see if she could smell it too; when she arrived, she perceived the wine slightly, but Val said it had started to fade away. Valerie called the friend that had given her the wine who happened to be visiting her own mother. Valerie asked for the phone number there and called them, but nothing was wrong there. A couple of days passed when she was speaking on the telephone to her Uncle Edward, on her father's side of the family. He had called Val to tell her that his son, Shane, had been carried to the hospital with chest pain. Valerie immediately exclaimed "OMG! Does he drink?" Her uncle said "no. Why?" As she told him about the strange smell of wine in her home, he broke in saying "you aren't going to believe this, but Shane and April, his wife, were trying out a wine-making kit and had just started making it. They had to quit when he started feeling bad. She carried him to the ER."

One premonition she received was for Valerie herself. She was supposed to drive to Huntsville, AL on business to meet her brother but called to cancel due to a wreck. "Where at?" he asked. She told him it hadn't happened yet but was supposed to occur when she drove down "so I'm not coming." Later that day, a friend stopped by Valerie's house after buying groceries and asked her "did you see that wreck down on the parkway?" Valerie asked her "was it an 18-wheeler going south just over the state line and a white SUV?" to which her friend replied, "yeah, did you see that?" Valerie answered "no." But she had because her car had been involved in the premonition of the wreck along with the other two vehicles.

Valerie and her mother have a gift; some might call it something else. All I know is if Val calls me about a premonition or bad feeling she's had of me, I will always listen and heed her warning...anyone else receiving a message from Valerie should pay attention as well.

THE MUSIC LESSON

A couple of years ago I received a message from my favorite English teacher, R.W. Groom, who reached out to me when he discovered I had become a paranormal investigator. It read "You do know about the old house that was behind the Episcopal Church, right?" I did not.

The house was used for music instruction in my hometown of Fayetteville, TN. Mr. Groom had taught guitar lessons there and wanted to let me know of an encounter he had had several years ago.

The story he told me was about a young lady who had recently married her sweetheart just before he joined the Confederacy. She would sit by the upstairs window watching and waiting for him to return while she played her violin. Some time had passed when news came about his death, and she fell into a deep depression. She stopped talking and only played her violin nightly in loneliness. Eventually, it was more than she could bear, and she hanged herself by tying a rope to the banister just outside her room, jumping to her death.

Mr. Groom met her one winter night after his last student left. He had closed his studio door to keep the heat in and heard violin music upstairs. Normally, he had the last lesson of the evening but thought perhaps the violin instructor was doing a make-up session with one of her students, so it didn't seem strange. After his student left and the doors were open, he listened for a while to the beautiful sound resonating throughout the grand old foyer.

Before leaving, he decided to say goodnight to the other teacher and started up the stairs. First, he noticed the temperature: each step became noticeably colder. It seemed there was a drop of fifteen to twenty degrees when he finally reached the door to her room. He called the instructor's name telling her he was leaving but got no response, only music. He repeated his words with the same results. As he raised his hand to knock, the music stopped, and a cold breeze blew by him. A strange feeling came over him, and he left without knocking.

The next time he saw the violin instructor, Mr. Groom asked her about her late lesson, and she only said "Oh, you met her. Was it cold? Could you hear the music?" and she told him the story of the lady in the house.

In later years, the house was blessed in order to wish the spirit peace before the building was demolished. To my knowledge, neighboring homes have not reported hearing the beautiful violin music, and it is believed the heartbroken spirit moved on. Perhaps she was finally reunited with her young husband for whom she so desperately waited and watched through the window as she tearfully played her violin.

Illustration inspired by *The Music Lesson*

THROUGH A NIGHTMARE

A friend of mine, Ernest, from high school, told me a story of an old house he and his wife, Anna, moved into and rented when they first got married. It had two stories; the upstairs was used primarily for storage, so they rarely went up there. The front door had a padlock on it that they secured whenever they left the property. Shortly after moving into their home, strange things began to happen: objects were moved that they hadn't touched; windows were opened; lights would be on that they had turned off before leaving the house. They usually dismissed these occurrences as simple forgetfulness.

The longer the couple stayed in the old house, the more bizarre the events became. They started hearing noises that often sounded like voices speaking, and strange bumping sounds came from the upstairs area. Around the same time, a very large, well-fed and healthy German Shepherd appeared and tended to hang around the house. The unusual stray had a collar but would not allow anyone to get close enough to see if there was an identification tag. No one claimed the shepherd.

Ernest fastened the padlock one evening and left the property to venture into town with Anna. Upon return, he unlocked the door and opened it for him and his wife to enter, but they were both startled by the dog running out of their home. Visibly shaken, they searched the house but because all the other openings were locked from the interior, could find no way the dog could have gotten inside. The activity in the old house increased including more noises clamoring without a visible source.

Shortly after, Anna was laid off from work and was alone in the house much of the time. She became so frightened with the ever-increasing interferences that she would call her parents to pick her up since the couple had only one vehicle at the time. She never told Ernest she was as scared as she was until after moving from the property a while later.

The turning point came one night after the couple had gone shopping in town. When they arrived home, they put the groceries in the kitchen and carried the remaining bags to the bedroom then retired for the evening. Once in bed, they heard movement from a bag and thinking it was a mouse, Ernest got up to take care of the problem; that's when more of the bags began to move as well, except there was no mouse.

Unable to determine the cause of the rustling bags, Ernest got back into bed. Immediately the house came alive with noises that lasted nearly an hour. Once the ruckus died down, the couple started hearing cows outside of their home. There was a gap at the bottom of the property's driveway that led into one of the neighbor's cow pastures; the cows shouldn't have been but were in the yard. The nervous herd had circled the house, and the animals were bellowing loudly.

Ernest went through the house peering out of the windows and found the home to be completely surrounded by cows. Returning to the bedroom, he looked out again and saw the strange German Shepherd pacing, and it appeared the herd was protecting the house and the couple from the dog. Able to keep the canine from getting to the house, the cattle left only after the dog had given up.

The next morning, Ernest and Anna visited their preacher even though they were afraid of what he might think. He listened to the couple's story, and after they described the night's events, he sat in deep thought before replying "I believe you." He advised them "greater is He that is in you, than he that is in the world." He told them to go back home and stand on God's promises. With their minds at ease, they both knew the preacher had spoken the truth.

A couple of weeks later, Ernest arrived home to find Anna scared to death. She asked if he had been upstairs lately, but he told her he had not. In tears,

Anna questioned if there was any way they could move from the old house. Ernest told her yes if that was what she really wanted. She then asked him to please look upstairs. Opening the door once he climbed the stairs, he found almost forty candles laid out on the floor in patterns. Neither Ernest nor Anna had put them there and had rarely even gone to the second floor. Ernest became scared as well and reported he never went back to open that door again.

Fortunately, an opportunity to buy their own house presented itself, and they were able to move out of the old house and off the troubled property. The house itself was later demolished to make room for an agricultural structure. Ernest and Anna live happily in their own home now but have never forgotten the frightening occurrences, remembering vividly each one.

STEP INSIDE HORNS CREEK

Horns Creek Baptist Church is an old, historic church near Edgefield, South Carolina featuring a big open room with an area for a pulpit. The ceiling features a large but strange motif in the center of the room. According to the historical marker, the church was organized in 1768 and incorporated in 1790. It sits in front of a creek that was once used for baptisms, and next to the building is a very old cemetery with intricate ironwork.

When Justine the only female with three other friends visited the historic church for a ghost hunt, it was rundown and not in very good shape, and it was empty inside. To try to contact any spirits there, she took a flashlight, tarot cards, and her glow-in-the-dark Ouija board. The board and planchette (oracle) would illuminate green in the darkness by shining a flashlight on it. She laid out a tarot deck and placed her board in the center of the big meeting room. Nothing happened for about an hour; it was a slow night. The group decided to step outside for a cigarette break, so Justine left the board in place with the oracle in the center. Someone in the group said into the empty room "if you're going to do something, do it now."

They were outside the church for ten to fifteen minutes then went back in to resume their investigation. What they found startled each one of them. The Ouija board was in the center of the floor exactly where Justine had left it; however, that was the only thing unchanged.

The planchette had been moved about three inches to the right, but the most startling evidence was a single shoe print in the middle of the still glowing board. The impression itself was evident because it was not luminescing as the board and oracle were. They weren't sure what that meant, except something weird had just happened while the investigators were outside.

One of the guys in the ghost hunting group started his spirit box to talk with the spirits there hopefully. One word "mother" was repeated three or four times, then the word "murder." Justine felt the words were directed at her since she was the only female, and feeling suddenly uncomfortable, they all decided to end the investigation and leave.

Vandals caused the old church to fall into more disrepair, and the sheriff's department had to begin making regular patrols checking on the property. The historical society took an interest in the church and fenced it up adding a caretaker's house so there would be someone on the property at all times. After much hard work from a team of volunteers, the church is looking much better and is even being used as a meeting house again. I wonder if the spirit who left a shoe print on Justine's Ouija board still visits the old church?

THE MIND IS A TERRIBLE THING

A couple of years ago I received an email from an older lady, Mary, from New York City, who now lives close to the Tennessee/Kentucky line. She had been experiencing unsettling disturbances for about eight months and had reached out to friends, family, and even her priest for help with the trouble, but no one could help her. She had a few medical problems that landed her in the hospital for several days for intense IV therapy, antibiotics, and pain medication. After her release, she returned home weak but healthier, and she felt much better. Once at home she began to notice an odd *static* around her body. She also began to feel a fingertip touch, then a strong hand that squeezed her foot and started traveling up her leg. She commented that it became a snakelike feeling wrapping up her leg and she would then suffer a sharp biting sensation; she called it the *Snake Spirit* and said the physical disturbances were very different than any she had ever experienced relating to her past illnesses and health problems.

Her daughter, MaryAnn, a Scientologist, prayed over Mary and smudged the home, but the relief only lasted three days. The older lady then contacted her Catholic priest, but he wouldn't offer any help. All she could continue to do was to pray. She feared the spirit was a demon sent to terrorize her for some reason, and she just wanted it gone. I called the older lady speaking to her, then spoke with her daughter to find out anything else related to the trouble. I also emailed a more thorough smudging ritual for the daughter to try.

I perceived from this connection, it was nothing demonic or dark, but something merely trying to get attention. I saw (in my mind's eye) a black figure about 3 feet in height at the lady's knee while she sat in her chair; it was the culprit of her pain, bites, stings, and static feeling. I discussed
with Mary the importance of keeping all negative emotions such as anger, sadness, and fear, at a minimum because the entity was feeding off them. She told me her daughter had also spoken of that importance and seemed to be relieved that what she'd already been told was legitimate.

During this time, I coordinated with a Nashville area team which was closer to Mary's home to do a walk-through of her location. The team historian did background property checks in New York and Tennessee without finding any outstanding information or what they believed pertinent to the case. They interviewed Mary and her daughter by phone, but after discussing her medical problems, they urged her to follow up with her doctor again. Unbeknownst to me, the team discarded any mention of the strange sensations the lady was suffering, and no property visit was made to see her or visibly search the location for anything paranormal.

About five days later, I got another voicemail from Mary begging me to phone her; she seemed distraught. Before I returned her call, I reached out to the other team to discuss the status. Speaking with Lou, the team founder, he told me that his team believed the problem was purely medical and had decided not to visit the lady but had spoken to her and her daughter by phone urging her to follow up with her doctor for more advice.

Unfortunately, what I could see was that the entity knew no one believed Mary and it was enjoying that. I knew something else was bothering her besides the medical signs and symptoms. I knew it; I felt it. The negative being was probably taking advantage of the situation. In a stronger individual, the spirit probably wouldn't even be acknowledged because of its low level. I discussed this aspect with Lou.

I didn't like the position in which I had been placed. My dilemma, to me, was complex. First, the lady had entrusted my team and me with her problems and was seeking advice and a resolution from us. Second, in turn, I had asked another team for help because they were closer to her location; unfortunately, I felt they had dropped the ball. Third, the lady was not going to stop calling me until I had some kind of solution or plan that she and her daughter could implement.

The founder stood by his team's decision that the occurrences were purely medical in nature but understood how helpless I felt about hot having any answers for the continued phone calls. I told him, I thought a medium could be brought in, and the only one I trusted was Mark Fults. Lou agreed Mark might be able to see what both of our teams had not, and in the process, offer a solution. He also thought speaking to Mark might be a better choice than to return the phone call to the older lady at the time.

I reached out to Mark, a psychic medium, and friend, for advice, sending him my notes and asking for help. He agreed to do a remote of the lady's home and property. The next day I received this response: "it's more medical and mental, not spiritual."

I felt lost for a second. What was that 3-foot tall black entity I had *seen* at the lady's knee bothering her? I asked Mark, and he wrote "her mental health." What did that mean? I asked him more questions. How had I seen a mental condition? How am I supposed to help anyone if I can't see things correctly? Mark answered "the mind of ill people is complex. It takes time." I asked him if I should speak with Mary one last time since she had messaged me again; I wondered if I should urge Mary to visit her doctor or should I talk with the daughter, MaryAnn? Mark suggested I speak with her daughter because it would be easier for her to understand the information and relay it to her mother. He told me the lady would not be happy and that I probably should avoid speaking directly to her about the findings.

I called MaryAnn and told her about my discussion with the other team and with Mark. She also knew her mother wasn't going to be pleased to hear we couldn't come to get rid of 'the spirit.' I urged her to find someone her mother could open up to - someone that she could speak to regularly. MaryAnn remembered a psychologist/therapist friend of the family her mother had always liked and knew she would talk to him. After ending the phone call with MaryAnn, I felt the tension ease from my own mind, and I realized Mary's sickness wasn't going to be allowed to reach any further; at least not through the phone lines to me ever again. After three years of silence, I pray that Mary and MaryAnn are both doing well.

REACHING THROUGH

EVP's co-founder Sean's grandparents were strict Southern Baptists. His maternal grandfather, a preacher, and his wife started well over 20 churches in Alabama and Southern Tennessee. Their beliefs focused on the Bible, following the commandments, Heaven being the destination of those that obeyed His word and Hell being where everyone else went after death. They definitely didn't believe in such things as ghosts; according to their belief, if something was allowed to roam the earth that was not alive, it most certainly was demonic. They didn't even allow Sean or his family to watch shows like *Dark Shadows* or anything related to the supernatural.

When Sean was about eight years old his mother and father divorced, and because his mother was in nursing school, Sean stayed at his grandparents' house often – enough, so he says they basically raised him. He was especially close to his grandmother. When Sean was in his early 20s, she was diagnosed with cancer, and he was heartbroken. The family didn't have much time to process her illness because she died after about only four months once the malignancy was discovered. Her passing was most unexpected because it was the grandfather who had been in poor health most of his later life.

When he was 24, about nine months after his grandmother's passing, Sean's grandfather became very sick, and hospice was called in to take care of the older man. It was all tough for Sean and the rest of the family to watch.

One night while asleep, Sean's grandmother came to him in a vivid dream to say "it's going to be okay. I've got him." He could hear her voice. It sounded like she was right in the room with him; in fact, the visit and conversation seemed so real to him, that he woke up in tears. His wife woke to find Sean distraught; concerned, she asked him what was wrong, but he was inconsolable. About a minute passed after Sean, and his wife woke up, then, at 3:00 AM the phone rang; it was Sean's mother calling to let him know his grandfather had just passed away.

What struck Sean the most, remembering his strict Baptist upbringing, was that if his grandparents didn't believe in the paranormal, how could his grandmother have come back to speak with him in a dream to let him know it was going to be all right? It made him think there was something more to what he had learned when growing up in the church. Maybe, just maybe, along with Heaven and Hell, your loved ones could reach out through dimensions to comfort you when it was most needed. Somehow, he believed that's exactly what had just happened. He felt very blessed to have gotten to speak with her once more, if even in a dream.

ABANDONED HOUSE

One dark night, a few of us decided to visit an old abandoned house on a gravel road out in the country. We'd heard several stories about a man in a top hat that would stand behind someone as they looked into the mirror. We went to search for that mirror and hoped to find the gentleman that liked to dress so formally.

We found the house in shambles, but at one time it must have been a lovely home. Strangely, whoever had lived there left a lot of their furniture behind. In the past, these belongings would have been stately, but the beautiful antiques with ornate wood carvings were now shattered and beyond hope of repair. Everything had fallen to ruin. It was sad.

This looked like the perfect setting for a horror movie. The front door stood permanently open for anyone to wander inside. The room to the left of the doorway was not safe to walk in since the floor had fallen through taking all the vintage pieces with it. There were piles of debris scattered from one side to the other. The only thing left standing was the old stone fireplace starting in the basement with a chimney stretching through the roof of the second floor.

To the right of the front door was some type of living area, perhaps a den or a library. The foyer itself was a long thin room stretching to the back of the original house with a staircase leading to the second floor. We'd walk through the room on the right to reach the dining room. There, a large heavy old walnut table stood in the center of the room. Old cabinets held nothing, but broken glass and the wallpaper was curling off the wall. On the far side of the table, you could see down into the basement several feet below.

Stepping carefully around the old floor, we would cut through the central doorway that opened back into the foyer to go upstairs. We climbed the staircase one person at a time. The railing leading up the stairs and around the top floor was long gone. Once upstairs, we found that someone had used the room to the left as a bedroom; there were still old mattresses there.

Across the upstairs hall, the room on the right had fallen all the way through so that you could see the first floor and the still-standing fireplace. There was another bedroom on the other side of the fireplace, with the bathroom that supposedly held the mirror you could stare into, but it wasn't safe to walk. Hopefully, Mr. Top Hat would join us somewhere else in the house.

Downstairs, we'd place our recorders and other instruments on the old walnut table to try to capture any spirit speaking to us. Our first investigation was creepy but relatively uneventful, and we knew we'd come back another time. Several months passed before we had a chance to return.

Walking through the front door for our second investigation, I noticed a little barn swallow had taken over the foyer entry light using the glass dome as her nest. She watched warily as we walked beneath her heading toward the dining room.

There were four of us there that night, and we found the furniture remnants to be in even more disrepair than our first visit. The table itself had fallen, and as I held up one side, Sean reached for a table leg, so he could replace it and set the table straight; only the leg jumped out of Sean's hands. I saw it. The table leg jumped out of his hands and went through the floor to the basement below.

'What just happened?" Sean asked a little surprised.

"I don't know" I answered as I shook my head.

"But did you see that?" he continued.

"Yes" spoken softly, "but I don't understand it. What just happened?"

Sean was shaking his head incredulously with eyebrows raised. "I don't know, but it felt like someone ripped the table leg from my hands and the next thing I knew it was in the basement. You saw it, right?" I had, and it would be something I'd replay in my mind over and over trying to figure it out. We could only prop the table up with an old chair after that, and so we did. We could then place our recorders and other instruments there.

The four of us decided to do an EVP session, and Sean got his video camera out to film. We began asking questions, hoping to get answers from the spirits, especially the man in the top hat. Suddenly the other male in our group quietly said, "something's touching me." Eerily as we looked, we could see two strands of his hair being lifted up by unseen hands. I quickly grabbed my digital camera to take pictures as Sean swung the video camera to focus on the weird sight, checking to make sure it was recording. We documented until the other guy said, "I need a break," and he walked through the room and out the front door. Sean followed him to show him the video; only the video wasn't there. Nothing had recorded in the entire session, and Sean was sure the camera was in good working order. In fact, once outside, the camera recorded easily. He came back inside to try to videotape again.

We started another session, but it was cut short when Sean asked for a sign from the spirits: "can you knock on the wall like this?" As he knocked twice. In the near darkness, lit only by flashlights, we received no knock in reply. But suddenly, a loud thud hit the foyer wall near the staircase. It rang out in the silence shattering our groups resolve to continue. It was time to leave. We had been warned.

Weeks later I visited the site alone one sunny afternoon. I walked around the property taking photos all the while feeling eyes watch me from inside and from the woods behind the old house. The barn swallow was gone, but the house looked just like we left it before.

Last year I heard that the old house had burned to the ground and decided to visit for myself one more time. It had indeed burned. All that was left was the bare-bones of the structure: front steps, concrete porch, basement rock walls, and the two old stone fireplaces still reaching up into the night sky.

All the beautiful pieces of furniture had turned to ash. The wraparound concrete porch now resembled a subway platform strangely out of place in the country. Looking down you could see rocks, ash and an occasional piece of metal left behind. The house was silent now, and only a feeling of sadness remained; any stronger sense of negativity had departed after the fire.

The house was gone. The sad remnants scattered.

But the woods behind the house site still stood watch.

Illustration inspired by *Abandoned House*

A LADY'S CHIFFEROBE

A good friend of mine, sensitive and empathic, Valerie, and her husband, Buck, own a store on the square in my hometown called Young Vintage & Antiques. About six months after opening their shop, Valerie found an old chifferobe at a yard sale. It was a good piece that had drawers on one side and a mirror on the other. Unfortunately, someone had painted it an ugly shade of turquoise, but not very well. It was a bad paint job.

"Oh! I want that! How much is it?" Valerie asked the owner. The answer was "five bucks." Valerie couldn't believe it and immediately said "really?" The lady explained "yeah. I'm just tired of it." Excited about her good luck, Valerie paid the money and told the woman that her husband would come to pick it up later that day.

Buck picked up the wardrobe then drove to the store and set it up there on display. Valerie found the mirror wasn't attached very well, so she removed it and placed it safely inside the door; that way it could still be seen but not get broken. The next day, the mirror was back on the door. Thoughtful, she again removed the mirror and replaced it once again inside. The following day, Valerie found the mirror once again returned to the door. She spoke aloud "okay, I'll leave it in the door."

A few days later a friend and sensitive, Adam, visited the store. He looked toward the old chifferobe and said "she doesn't like it - the lady. She doesn't like the paint. Somebody messed with her furniture." Valerie had already sensed just that.

The shop owners would place objects to sell on display on or next to the old chifferobe only to find them moved further away the next day. Several shoppers admired the antique saying "this is nice" but would walk away. No one would buy the chifferobe even though the price was set at only sixty dollars.

Valerie decided to post a photo of the antique on social media at a reduced price. She listed the wardrobe with the caption "first person to come by the store and give twenty dollars can have it." A woman soon came in and paid the fee. Relieved, Valerie asked her what she planned to do with it and was told: "I'm gonna redo it and get that ugly paint off of it then use it for my daughter's clothes." Valerie thought that was a good idea and told the buyer "that'll be really nice."

Springtime came, and Valerie pulled into the driveway of a yard sale in progress. Inside the garage against one wall, she saw the same chifferobe she had sold a few months before. No changes had been made; it still had the same ugly painted turquoise finish. Turning to the face she remembered, Valerie asked "so, are you going to redo it?" But the woman shook her head and said "no. I've decided we're probably just going to sell it. I don't know what it is about that thing, but I don't like it in the house." Valerie told her "that might be a good idea," when the lady shot her a strange look but kept silent.

Maybe, if someone finally strips that ugly paint from the antique and lovingly restores it to the beautiful piece it once was, maybe just maybe, the lady that is attached to it can find peace. Had something happened in the last house to the woman who bought the old chifferobe? Had something happened to her daughter? Had objects somehow moved by themselves away from the antique? We probably will never know these answers, but the odd expression the woman gave Valerie may have been the only one needed.

THE GRAVEL ROAD

One of my good friends and Elk Valley Paranormal teammate, Matthew, has seen, heard and experienced unexplained happenings all of his life. He had been asking me for weeks if I'd driven down a particular road out in the country he described as weird, maybe even ominous, and wanted to get my reaction or reading of the spot.

My team Elk Valley Paranormal was just finishing a public hunt when Matthew asked if I had time to follow him to the gravel road that evening; I did. We also asked Sean, EVP's Co-founder, to come with us and he agreed. We each got into our separate vehicles and headed south with Matthew leading, followed by me, then Sean bringing up the rear.

We drove down the highway eventually turning off onto another well-traveled road in the county and kept driving. As we rounded a sharp curve, I watched Matthew drive slowly across a fog encased bridge. His headlights suddenly illuminated a man who walked directly in front of his car but disappeared halfway across. Stunned, I instinctively slowed to a crawl as I crossed the same bridge and saw Matthew continue driving away from the bridge and the man. I frantically looked from side to side seeing no man - no one - no one anywhere.

Immediately grabbing my phone, I reached Matthew by speed dial. "Matthew! What happened back there?" He replied "It felt like my car was driving through water; being pushed back. It knows we're coming." I asked him if he'd seen a man on the bridge to which he merely told me "No." That was impossible! "Matthew, he walked right in front of your car! I thought you were about to hit him, but he just disappeared!" I heard a new interest in his voice, "You're kidding! There was nobody there! Just a feeling of being pushed back." We soon hung up but continued toward our destination already knowing the night was a strange one.

Coming to a crossroads, we turned right and drove a short distance before coming to a gravel road onto which we turned. My phone rang. It was Sean saying, "Where are we going?" All I could tell him was the only thing I knew: "Where Matthew wants us to go." Then, a little impatiently, he asked: "Where is it?" But I didn't really know. "Calm down! He says it's a really weird spot and he doesn't want to tell us anything about it to see if either of us can figure out exactly where it is." Sean persisted, "How much further?" In that second, I was struck with a strange awareness. "Sean, I feel it. We're getting closer." and on the other end of the phone I heard "Oh, hell." then "what is it?" I hung up the phone quickly with "It's here. It's right here. I gotta hang up. Bye."

I didn't know what it was, but I knew it was watching us. Slowly we neared another bridge then crept across it. Looking to each side, all I could see was a typical country stream bounded by trees and brush; nothing out of the ordinary, but it really wasn't ordinary. It was... different. There was a feeling of something ominous, watchful, and the air was thick somehow. A slight chill went up my spine as I felt unseen eyes hiding somewhere near the bridge and I couldn't shake the feeling.

After crossing the bridge and traveling down the gravel road, we reached pavement and continued driving, turning left, then left again. My phone rang and answering it, I heard Sean say, "Now where are we going?" I told him to just keep following Matthew.

Soon a church came into view, and we all pulled into the parking lot as the first drops of rain began to gently fall. Matthew and I rolled down our windows at the same time and he just looked at me expectantly. "The bridge" is all I said as he nodded. Sean got out of his car asking what it was. "The bridge." I repeated, "Didn't you feel it? Something was there that didn't want us there." Again, Matthew nodded and stood up from his opened car door. The three of us stood talking a few seconds then the sky opened up; hard rain falling straight down soaking our clothes as we ran to stand under the church pavilion. We talked excitedly about the night's experiences until each started to get cold from soaked clothes.

We agreed the gravel road bridge was a weird place, but I was the only one who saw a man walk directly in front of Matthew's car earlier, and Matthew was the only one who experienced a strange resistance on himself as well as his vehicle. We may never know who or what is at that bridge, but we do know it's there waiting and watching, or maybe guarding something of which we probably want no part. I've not traveled the road again since that night, but even though it is slightly out of the way to drive in the area, I attribute my absence to something more uncomfortable - something that really doesn't want humans near. Maybe, just maybe subconsciously I've agreed to stay away.

TAINTED LAND

About five years ago a friend, Todd, contacted Justine knowing she studied Wicca and practiced the old studies of witchcraft. He told her there was a lot of crazy stuff happening on his property and had been going on for a long time. She had asked him to explain in more detail. Todd lived with his parents, and he told her the house had lots of noises and disturbances including growls and doors slamming. He continued telling her plates and glasses were flying off the shelves, and they had all seen shadowy figures in plain sight. Also, one of the more disturbing things Todd reported was that animals (livestock) had been found dead - two were found decapitated with their heads lying near the bodies. Todd told her he knew the mutilations weren't caused by another animal, a hunter, or even a friend playing a very sick joke. He also reported twice that vehicle roofs had been caved in, and he was frightened enough to call Justine saying, "this *Thing* did it all."

Going in, Justine knew one witch wasn't going to be enough to take on some ancient entity that, if true, could rip heads off animals. She went to see what the problem was, taking Samantha, a medium she had worked with and trusted, her husband Donatien (Don), and another person that claimed to be a medium. Justine said that she knew she'd have to go back with more powerful people the next time if she found out the entity was indeed ancient.

Driving onto the property on August 22, 2013, Justine and her husband the skeptic, both began feeling something that she described as an "instant creep factor." She explained that whatever it was made their "guts twist up inside," and hair stood up all over their bodies.

Gathering with the two mediums and Todd, Justine spoke with them about what they were about to do. She asked the medium she had never worked with to stand back, watch the ritual and learn. Don did not participate in the ceremony staying away while Justine and the other three walked into the woods.

With her, Justine carried her tools: salt, sage, candles, crystals and stones, witch's holy water, and feathers along with her Book of Shadows. The salt and sage were to purify and protect the area for what about to perform the ritual. Witches holy water is water that has sat under a full lunar cycle, one month. Justine set up her altar with the items as a type of offering: placing charcoal and iron as elements to ground them to the earth; a black and a white candle for banishment and purity respectively; and feathers to represent air and truth.

Justine called a full circle for protection: the four corners North, South, East, West; and the elements Earth, Air, Fire, Water. Setting the circle up so that nothing could come in that she did not allow.

Justine spoke: "I call upon the Guardian of the East and the Element of Air. Bring to our sacred space your wisdom and understanding. Enlighten us with your knowledge. I call upon the Guardian of the North and the Element of Earth. Bring to our sacred space your power and strength. You are the rock that we stand on. I call upon the Guardian of the West and the Element of Water. Bring to us the truth and reality of all that we seek. I call upon the Guardian of the South and the Element of Fire. Bring to us your fierceness and power of destruction.

She continued "Watch over us and protect us this night, as we will be with unwelcome spirits. As we perform this rite, keep our hearts pure and our minds clear; keep our bodies strong and our minds focused. You will be needed and are welcomed."

She saged everyone before bringing them into the ring to purify them and prepare them for the event. Reciting a blessing, she then drew a star on each person's forehead with holy water and finally kissed each one. Todd exclaimed "ow!" Saying the kiss had burned, hurting him.

Once the four of them were safely inside the boundary, Justine closed the circle so that nothing else could enter. Everything in the light (the circle) was protected.

"By my words and our presence and our protectors of old - I have consecrated this space and made it sacred ground. For those whose hearts and actions are impure or malevolent...both earthly, eternal or spiritual - you may not send your impure energy or beings acting on your behalf. This space is protected until the gods of old depart and release it. Furthermore, the participants of this rite are also protected going forward.

Then speaking loudly so as not to appear weak, she announced her pagan name: "I am Lady Edana Storm" (Edana is Celtic for fire). "I am not afraid. I have come with a gentle and understanding heart. I have also come with a fierce and powerful will."

She continued to speak saying she wanted to learn who or what was there and if some resolution could be reached. "I understand you have been provoked and disturbed by those with less power and impure intentions; however, this is not the purpose of this rite. We are here to understand. Make no mistake by my gentle intentions; I am prepared for you. I will remind all beings that have approached - earthly, ethereal or those on behalf of others - you may not enter this sacred space."

Calling to the spirit, she demanded the entity speak to her "I ask you now - declare yourself to me. Tell me your name and state your purpose."

The entity began to talk through Samantha the medium in a deep guttural voice. It was insulting using foul language, vulgarities and laughing at Justine, but she told it she wasn't afraid because she was well protected.

Several times Justine told the evil spirit to leave and said it was not welcome and must leave the grounds and the family, but the being laughed at her and repeated that it "*was called.*" She spoke to it saying "your presence is disrupting their lives as well as their loved ones. We ask you to leave this area. Rest yourself. Let go of your anger towards them and this area." She continued "Those that have caused you ill will be punished when the time is right. Recede to the realm you belong in or to an uninhabited area never to return. Be at peace." As she demanded it not hurt the family, it still laughed.

Justine read a spell in Latin and followed it with "It is time to leave here; all is well. There is nothing here for you now. You must be gone. Go now, complete your passing with our blessing – Farewell. Farewell."

After the reading of the Latin spell, the entity's voice coming through Samantha had changed from guttural to a more acceptable tone and told them it had *"been called"* there and was *"not leaving."* When the spirit would not participate anymore, it disappeared, and in the distance, they heard a growl. She knew it would not speak to the group further that night, so she closed the circle reversing everything and thanking the elements.

"Spirits of Goodness, Spirits of Light,
Protect us from all plight
Protect us from danger
Protect us from harm
Let us be safe, secure and charmed
Charmed and protected
Safe from pain
May we walk in sunshine
Sheltered from the rain
Spirits of Goodness, Spirits of Light
Please protect us with all your might."

Afterward, a friend told Justine that area was owned by a wealthy slave owner who coerced many people to come to work his land in exchange for granting their freedom once they completed their tasks. He never freed any of his slaves; he killed them instead.

Justine feels the entity was ancient and well connected to the grounds. She believes Santeria slave practitioners called it as vengeance on the owner of the slaves.

Justine's original teacher of tarot, spells, and rituals said it might be possible to gather with a large group of well-established witches and charge the entity into a large piece of quartz to bind it; however, it is dangerous and could end up going into something or someone instead, so that has not been attempted.

DROP ZONE

Several years ago, while living in Arizona, I was told of a bizarre sighting on an Air Force drop zone near my home. The person who mentioned it to me, Jack Assante, asked if I'd like to visit but wouldn't say exactly what the strange thing was. He did say we could easily sneak onto the one-mile square military property since he had just landed a couple of jumps in the area, and I don't know why, but I agreed to go.

We climbed into his truck, and Jack drove us a few miles turning into an area with a metal gate that had been left unlocked, so we went right in leaving the gate open. Winding through tumbleweeds, cacti, and rocks, Jack drove telling me a little about his jumps, but as for what he wanted to show me, well, he kept me guessing. He said we were driving straight to the spot he wanted me to see and then cryptically "you'll know it when you see it."

The desert area was eerily quiet except for the truck motor and the tires crunching over the terrain. We had been driving for a few minutes taking a series of left turns when Jack said seemingly to himself "where did it go?" I felt a sinking feeling in the pit of my stomach for whatever reason had caused Jack to question himself. I scooted forward in the seat to try to see the area better, not really knowing for what I was looking. My heart was beating faster, and I began wishing I was anywhere but there with Jack. Why had I agreed to this expedition? Stupid curiosity! This outing was meant to be fun, harmless excitement, but suddenly felt dangerous.

"There it is!" He exclaimed as I snapped my head around in the direction he pointed. Strange shapes - what was it? Leaving the manual truck in park but still running, we got out and walked toward the odd scene. Oh no! As I stared, at the horse, calf, and two goats, all dead and mutilated, I heard Jack say "they were standing up earlier with props. Somebody's pushed them over." This wasn't a good situation; it wasn't good at all. We were not in a safe place.

I could see the insides of the poor creatures were gone entirely leaving only the outer layer of animal hide. They had been butchered and burned, perhaps sacrificed. It felt wrong being there now, and suddenly I felt watched. Looking around, I spotted a white van about 100 yards from us just sitting there. We had been alone as far as I knew when we entered the drop zone. From what direction had the vehicle come? How had we not heard any noise coming from it? And why was it just sitting there?

I urgently told Jack "we've got to go now!" We rushed to the truck and jumped in noting the van had started driving in our direction. Jack slammed the stick shift into first pulling away from the ruins. The gate was now over a half mile away. Turning left, he sped up the truck. Watching over my shoulder, I saw the van was gaining on us. "Who are they?" I asked. In a hushed voice, Jack simply said: "I don't know." He took a breath and then finished with "I don't think I want to know." I knew I didn't.

The metal gate finally came into sight, but now was closed. We had purposely left it open when we drove through, so we didn't have to get out and open it again. Someone in the white van closed it, and now we knew, they didn't want us here. Were those the people who had tortured those animals? I felt the answer was *yes*. Suddenly I realized these people in the white van were most likely part of a cult I'd heard rumors of in the area; a group of people that worshiped Satan and sacrificed animals to him.

The van was within 50 feet of us as Jack rammed the stick into neutral and yelled "quick! Drive! As soon as it's open, go through! I'll catch up to you!" Adrenaline kicked into high gear as I slid across the seat grabbing the wheel, clutching it into first gear and flooring the gas stirring a cloud of dust behind the truck. Rushing through the now open gate and slowing long enough for Jack to wrench open the passenger door, jump in and yell "GO! GO!" as I floored it again.

We were both sweating and breathing fast as we roared away from the drop site. Jack turned to watch out of the back window as I often glanced in the rearview waiting for the white van to reappear. Luckily, it never did. Just in case though, I wove us through several streets in a random pattern before feeling safe enough to pull into my driveway.

Afterward, Jack apologized for the trip becoming dangerous, saying he had no idea it would turn out as scary as it did. I was just glad to be away from the drop zone. He told me a few weeks later, after parachuting into the area, the animal carcasses had been completely removed leaving nothing behind but scorched earth. I never went back and never cared to return.

UNINVITED

My childhood friend, Emily, called me for help with a problem plaguing her family, especially her daughter Briley who I'd met at my old dance studio when I taught there. She said she didn't think the disturbances were Briley's imagination because they'd all experienced something where they lived, even her skeptical husband.

The land was Emily's maternal grandparents with a branch of water that runs close to the two houses on the property; also, there is a cemetery there where all her relatives are buried. Her parents' house is the closest to the main road, and Emily and her husband built directly behind that one.

The first strange incident that happened after the new house was built occurred in May 2009. Emily and her mother were upstairs painting the walkthrough that leads from the media room over the garage to the two bedrooms and one bath on the other side. Lydia turned to look at her daughter, smiled and motioned behind her; she thought Briley was sneaking up on them trying to scare them, but her granddaughter wasn't there.

Howie, Emily's husband, was in the downstairs den when he heard "hey!" at the stairs which caused him to leave. He's also *heard* their daughter upstairs before when Briley's not there but doesn't like to admit it could be something paranormal.

In March 2010, Briley moved into the upstairs of the house. One day she heard talking downstairs, and because she was supposed to be alone, went down the steps with her bow and arrow thinking there was an intruder; but the television and radio were both off, and there was no one else inside.

One night Emily was alone with only the dog, Buddy, who she reports stood on his hind legs then started charging at something while looking up at the ceiling; she couldn't see anything there. They have taken several photos and have found orbs in many of them. Occasionally they all smell smoke and the scent of something burning, but her husband only smokes outside the house. Later, during a night when the moon was full, Emily was walking across the yard from her home to her mother's when she noticed something bizarre. All the cows were in a straight line watching Lydia's house. She heard a cough and smelled snuff which no one in her family currently uses; however, her late maternal grandmother did.

Two years ago, during a tornado, the ladies were in the storm shelter between the houses. Afterward, they went inside Lydia's house to find the hallway phone, a landline, was the only one working, but more strange, was that all the pictures in the hallway had been placed immediately below where they had been hanging. They believe they were put on the floor because if the tornado had caused them to blow off the wall, they would have been scattered on the floor and broken instead of neatly lying right up against the bottom of the wall unscathed.

On another occasion, Briley was taking a shower, and she heard breathing on the other side of the shower curtain. Briley refers to the spirit's presence as "her." No one was there. Afterward, she went downstairs to wash dishes and feels like she slipped into a sort of trance. She remembers looking up from the sink to see out the kitchen window in front of her. Something headless was walking through the backyard holding an object in its hand, and when she blinked, it was closer to the house than it should have been, moving unnaturally fast. She was crying hysterically when her mother came in from work.

Later, Briley was terrified by something wrapping dark "fingers" around the side of the doorway leading from the upstairs walkthrough into the bedroom in which she sleeps. She reports she slept downstairs on the couch that night. She also says she has heard someone coming toward her and her dog while she watches television, but no one is there.

Just before midnight one evening, Briley went upstairs to her bedroom after lying downstairs on the couch for a while. Emily told me the dog just couldn't get settled that night for some reason. After she went to bed herself, her phone rang; it was a very distraught Briley calling from upstairs to come to help her. Emily ran upstairs to find Briley cowering under the covers and crying. She told her mother after she had laid down, she felt something crawl up onto the bed coming all the way up to her right side settling there. She said she heard something "clearing its throat" and reports she couldn't open her eyes or move the right side of her body at all until her mother came upstairs to check on her.

When Emily contacted me, she told me a few things that were going on, and we set a date for a walk-through. Right after that, she went onto the screened-in back porch to make sure the blinds were up and found something a bit disconcerting: a glass lantern they had hanging on a hook there, was sitting on the floor. No one had been out there at the time. The lamp was turned around but not broken. She reported it looked like someone took it off the hook and set it down out there.

I did a walk-through of the home one afternoon with one of my EVP teammates, Justine, and spoke with Emily and Briley upstairs where most of the disturbances took place. We all found the second floor to be heavier and had a feeling of being watched. To put them more at ease, I encouraged them to repeat aloud *The Lord's Prayer* and the *23rd Psalms* every night (or as often as they wished), as well as provided them with a prayer to the Archangels to recite for peace and protection:

> *Michael to my right*
> *Uriel to my left*
> *Raphael in front of me*
> *Gabriel behind me*
> *Heaven above me*
> *Earth below me*
> *I am protected*

We decided a house cleansing ritual would be best to tame the disturbances instead of a full-blown investigation. Immediately after we'd agreed on a time and day, my grounding and protection bracelet broke sending gemstone chips flying all over the hardwood floor. We spent several minutes picking up as many as we could find. I never like to leave anything at an investigation for fear there may be an energy tether linked to myself that a spirit could follow.

When we went back to perform the cleansing, Emily and Briley returned to me the last few pieces of my bracelet they found after Justine and I left on our first visit. We began the smudging ritual outside the garage since that is the way they usually enter the house, smudging Howie first, then Emily and Briley before Justine and I walked inside chanting continuously. Howie went to smoke outside while we were in the home performing what he called "hocus-pocus." Emily and Briley had already gone through the entire house opening every cupboard, drawer, and door so that we could move faster. We entered the laundry room off the garage and then walked clockwise through one side of the kitchen and den then up the steps.

Upstairs again was heavier and moving still in the direction of the clock, we turned left to go around the second bedroom and the bathroom there, then down the north side of Briley's bedroom into the walk-through. In the media room, we concentrated extra smoke around the steps that led down into the garage. Finishing there, we went back moving clockwise into Briley's bedroom, back down the stairs, completing the den and entered the master suite. Back out into the dining room, we walked onto the enclosed back porch, finishing the north side of the kitchen and finally back out to the garage. I again smudged Briley and Emily, followed by Justine, and then she performed the chant and ritual over me. Before leaving, I told them, we could come back if needed to complete a more thorough cleansing and blessing if the disturbances didn't calm down. The next day Briley texted me that she had spent the night downstairs last night "just in case because she didn't need any of that stress" before morning referring to any further paranormal disturbance following the smudging. She told me they slept fine and had said all the prayers.

A few months later, I ran into Briley and asked her how everything was going. She said there had been no problems but wanted to tell me what had happened to her skeptical father. It seems after Justine, and I left the property, Howie was laughing at his wife and daughter for having someone come out to the house and perform some "silly hocus-pocus demonstration" He made fun of the entire situation, in particular, any spirit, because he did not believe in anything paranormal. He went outside to smoke and heard someone call his name which freaked him out. Thinking either Emily or Briley had said it, Howie came back inside and confronted them about trying to scare him. They didn't know what he was talking about and told him he'd better be more careful and not make fun of it ever again. That freaked him out even more.

After Howie's comeuppance, he prefers not to speak about anything paranormal, especially as it relates to his own home; in fact, Briley reports he hasn't even uttered the word *ghost* since hearing his name called. So far, the disturbances have disappeared and hopefully, won't bother the family again - at least as long as Howie behaves.

ATTACHMENTS

My husband and I have been married just over five years now. When I moved into his 'bachelor pad,' we began making it our family home: him, me, and as soon as we finished moving everything in, my cat, Bella, who was then at my Mother's house. When we had time, we'd move a few more boxes and unpack them. It took several months before Bella joined us. During that time, I discovered something interesting about my new home: it already had a pet. To be exact, we had the spirit of a cat living with us.

The first time I noticed it, I was almost asleep. My husband, an early bird, had already fallen asleep a couple of hours before. While drifting off, I felt Bella jump up onto the bed at my feet. She started delicately stepping in a small circle until she decided which direction to face, and then she settled down. Smiling sleepily, I closed my eyes. Then suddenly, I remembered Bella wasn't living with us yet! I knew I

Illustration inspired by *Attachments*

hadn't imagined anything; I most definitely sensed a cat now lying quietly at my feet. Relaxing, I smiled again and slept.

The cat didn't jump onto the bed every night, but she did often enough that I could point it out to my husband when it happened, and he understood what I meant. He told me of a few times he had felt the sensation of something close to the foot of the bed. We both got used to the company.

On one of our first vacations as a married couple, we traveled to Lake Erie then went through Ohio to the western portion of Pennsylvania to visit my husband's extended family. He showed me where he'd lived and gone to school as well as places he had been, all the while telling me stories of his childhood. He introduced me to the family he missed after moving to Tennessee when he was fifteen. During our trip, we enjoyed visiting his relatives of both parents then drove to Pittsburgh for the evening. It was there I was hit with a terrible case of food poisoning that sent me to bed for the next twenty-four hours. When I began feeling a little better, we continued our vacation driving across the state to Lancaster and then later on to Valley Forge.

It was very hot the day we visited the historical park, and still not feeling my best, I had to sit down often to rest. We made our way to the visitor's center museum, and I found a bench to sit on inside the air-conditioned building while my husband brought the truck closer. When it was time to leave, we got in the vehicle and drove toward Philadelphia. There, I finally started feeling much better, so we were able to walk around touring the historic areas and even ate a Philly cheese steak before leaving the city. Heading south, we drove through Shenandoah National Park admiring the beautiful scenery, then headed back to Tennessee. When we got home, we unpacked and settled back into our normal routines.

It wasn't long before I realized we had someone else in the house with us. One afternoon alone, I heard a strange rustling sound, but I couldn't pinpoint it. I got my digital recorder out and turning it on, I walked from room to room saying "I know you're here because I can hear you moving, but I can't see you." Going back into one of the rooms I said, "I'm turning the light on now." Upon review of my recording at that exact moment, the electronic voice phenomenon I caught was a Class A: meaning you could easily hear and understand it with your own ears. The voice said, "thank you."

Excited about the Class A evp, I asked many more questions dowsing with copper rods and recording everything. I discovered a nurse had attached to me while I was still not feeling well at Valley Forge and came all the way back home with us trying to help me feel better. I was genuinely surprised and touched, thankful she had cared enough to look after me.

The nurse stayed for several months with us and our spirit cat. I began to sense she needed to move on but was unsure if she should. I talked with my friend, Penny, who told me to thank the spirit then wish her home and I did.

Afterward, I guess it was a few weeks later, I realized we hadn't had our ghost cat jump onto the bed in a while. I kept waiting, but it never happened again. It seems the nurse and the cat became buddies, so when she left the cat did as well.

My cat, Bella, has since become the little lady of the house. She occasionally jumps up onto the foot of the bed after my husband leaves in the early morning for work, but she prefers another area. Her favorite spot is a window seat where she can watch the birds and squirrels on the feeders outside and then she peacefully naps in the sun coming through the glass.

Once in a while, I think about the sweet nurse and the phantom cat. Did she return to Valley Forge taking the cat with her? Hopefully, they were able to cross over when I wished the nurse home. I sincerely hope they've found the perfect destination and can now rest in forever peace. I just would like for them to know that while they lived in my home, they each brought happiness and a feeling of wonder that I will never forget.

LYNCHBURG HAUNTED HOME

The history of the Lynchburg Haunted Home at 250 Main Street in Tennessee is confusing, to say the least; no one is really sure when it was built. Some say the building was started sometime during the 1800s and was used as a Civil War Hospital. Others state it wasn't erected until possibly as late as 1920 and was used as a boarding house before it was a funeral home. In 1934, it became Harrison's Funeral Home owned by Charles Leo Harrison and his wife, Christine. They had a son Charles Kenneth. The old building has expanded over the years with a few additions being added causing it to morph into an odd collection of interconnected rooms; besides the main house, there is a basement, storage areas, the garage, and an embalming room. One addition built onto the south side of the house was made into an apartment. The property as of 2018 is for sale at $1.25 million.

From 2014 up through October of 2017, the owner hosted a haunted house for the Halloween season with the help of volunteers led by Adam Head, founder of Dark Specter Paranormal Research. My friend Justine says they needed help to run the attraction, so she invited two friends from Augusta to drive up in exchange for food and a place to stay. Before they arrived, Justine asked the owner for a private investigation for the small group after the haunted house was shut down for the night; he agreed.

They started their hunt in the boy's bedroom upstairs and didn't have any paranormal activity, so they moved to the room next to the locked one where the old lady died. Her bedroom remains closed for most investigations. Justine placed her flashlight securely on the windowsill in the room as they sat in the center of the floor. She reports that the energy in the old house suddenly felt "off." It was at that time they all heard footsteps climbing the stairs. The steps came all the way to the top floor, but no one was there that they could see. Immediately the flashlight flew off the window, and the spirit box said "suicide." Jackson, from Augusta, started crying uncontrollably and said his thoughts had been of members of his family. They believed something had manipulated his thoughts into thinking very negative ideas toward his family members.

Justine reports trying every known way to debunk the flashlight flying off the windowsill but knows because they were all sitting down, none of them could have jarred it enough to make it move; she also remembers checking and finding the window shut tight and no draft was coming in. No viable reason for the torch's movement was ever discovered, and to this day, she still recounts the story with wonder.

***

I also have a flashlight story from the old haunted home. I went to a public investigation hosted by Dark Specter Paranormal Research (Founder Adam Head) in June of 2014 with a few of my friends one night, carrying my recorder, and had my flashlight attached by carabiner at my hip. This public hunt was open, meaning each person was allowed to walk through certain rooms of the old house alone without a guide leading the way. We had been upstairs, and then started touring the downstairs areas when we came to what we had been told was a waiting area outside two unfinished bathrooms.

We were walking from room to room, and as we went into and out of the unfinished right side heading to the other, I felt a sudden slap as my flashlight hit my right thigh and flew apart. I wasn't sure what had happened, but Lynn, the man behind me, said: "dropped your batteries."

"Aw, man!" laughing, I looked down to see them on the floor. As my teammate Melinda, handed me the batteries, I received an evp. Upon later audio analysis, I heard "You suck." I'm not sure at who it was directed but feel they were speaking to Melinda for helping me. Something was there they didn't want me to see, or they didn't want me there at all.

But where were the rest of the flashlight pieces? I asked "Now, where's the piece that holds the batteries in? And the whole top of the light went flying." The evp captured at that precise moment was "they're outside."

Lynn handed me what he'd just found on the floor, the piece that snapped to keep the batteries inside, and commented "That was kinda weird. You didn't do anything. It just exploded on ya!" All I could say was "I know, right?" as I kept looking for more parts.

The next evp recorded said "I can't see!" and then "She hasn't seen one thing."

Melinda picked something up and said, "Is this it?" It was the top that screwed onto the body of the flashlight, but where was the little silver piece that held the bulb?

Aloud I asked, "Who didn't want me to come in here?" with an answered evp "She's back."

Suddenly Melinda said, "Got something on my arm. You have a flashlight? Shine it right here." That moment's evp said "Hey! Shut up!" but we didn't hear it live. Melinda kept explaining "Something touched my arm when I had it right here." But all I could do was hold up my not-quite-complete flashlight and say laughingly "Well, I would, but..." making us both laugh.

That's when Lynn realized I still didn't have all the pieces of my light and he said "Oh! You need that whole part of your flashlight?" Nodding, I said "Yeah, the light." And he replied, "That's the main part!" Yes, it was, and I still was looking around in the dark for it. He moved around me looking at the floor again. Into the room, I commented, "They did it on purpose."

Melinda was now looking harder for the light and Lynn moved out into the waiting area. "Surely it didn't go that way," I said to Lynn while still searching the incomplete room. Melinda was now looking harder for the light, and Lynn explained from just outside the bathrooms "I thought it might have rolled up in here."

"Where? Do you see it?" I asked. On audio, I'd later find someone saying, "it might throw." Something definitely hit my flashlight scattering all the pieces.

Melinda had walked out to look with Lynn when she leaned down and said: "there's something down here, but I can't tell…" I rushed out to see where she was pointing: the last piece! The silver dome that held the bulb had somehow flown left outside the room to rest underneath the slight overhang of the step-down. It should have either been in the same place where the incident happened, and the other pieces were found, or it should have flown out the door a few feet away from the step-down. Instead, it was right up against the wall under the slight overhang of the step-down, and it wasn't found until we had stepped out of the bathroom area, back out into the waiting room and looked back towards the bathroom. There it was on the floor up against the wall, as if someone had hidden it from me.

"Yeah! Yeah!" I exclaimed, and Lynn agreed "there ya go!" Laughing, I said to everyone in the room "somebody really didn't want me to see," and Lynn agreed. As I struggled with the parts, Melinda offered to hold them until I could fit everything back together.

Lynn was still shaking his head "you didn't drop it. It exploded! It like literally flew off her hip!" he said to everyone around.

All I could say was "It was weird" as I finished piecing the light together. I received an evp that said, "They're coming back" and "That f**king bothers me."

"Let's see if I have everything together right" flipping the switch and seeing my flashlight once again shine. Lynn repeated, "There ya go!"

"Yep!" I exclaimed and continued "So I'm gonna look around anyway Mr. Ghost!" We all laughed as we continued our hunt. The last evp in that section was "she's funny."

We couldn't replicate any of that flashlight incident, and it remains somewhat of a mystery. But I do know that the spirits wanted the light, and maybe me, gone.

PARANORMAL EMAIL

In September of 2015, I received a text message from a troubled girl who wanted me to help her understand the voices she was hearing. She said she was being followed. I replied with my email address, and she sent a video; unfortunately, the audio was not included, so I was not able to hear any electronic voice phenomenon (evp). I could only tell her I saw nothing paranormal in her evidence.

She then emailed several clips from separate rooms in her apartment and even one from her parked car. There was only one I couldn't use because she had the radio on and it was too close to her recorder. I reached in pulling out one evp from each of the other clips and emailed the deciphered messages back to her.

I shut down my computer for the night, and without going into detail, my husband and I had an argument that evening, but we were able to come to an agreement before the night ended.

During this time, the girl sent me a short email with another audio clip attached. I opened it the next evening and began analyzing the clip. The first evp I was able to obtain called the girl by name, said they wanted her out of their house and asked if she would leave.

Then I heard the second message, but this one was different. This one spoke directly to me. They called me by name and talked about the argument we had had the night before. They said they could help me fix the problem if I would just visit them. I couldn't breathe. In fact, I freaked out enough to tell my husband even though he usually doesn't get involved with any of my paranormal pursuits. He couldn't quite understand them, and he didn't understand what had happened. I couldn't understand what had happened either. I saved everything I had, and after emailing the girl her message, not mine, I stopped working for the night. In my reply email, I told her I would not be able to help her further.

The next day the girl sent me another email begging me to speak with her brother who is a policeman because finally, she had someone who believed her. Her brother, like others around her, thought her complaints were all in her head. Reluctantly, I told her he could call me.

Soon after I received a phone call from the officer, who was incredulous - mostly because his sister finally had a form of validation no one else had offered. He told me of the many police reports she had made over the last several months of harassment and stalking which no one could prove. Although his belief made him extremely skeptical, he realized there was more to his sister's complaints than merely an overactive imagination or need for attention.

The results I found clearly showed the girl was being bullied by a couple of intelligent spirits. They also knew no one believed her and found that entertaining. The worst part was that the girl could see the entities, but she thought they were living people following her and she saw them everywhere and daily. Her family thought she was out of her mind and unfortunately those spirits were pushing her closer to insanity.

The officer and I had a long conversation over the reports I had emailed his sister and what could be done. He asked if I could travel there, but it was too far. I suggested an area paranormal team that could perform a smudging ritual using white sage and advised prayers for the Archangels to protect his sister. I can only hope they carried out my advice for the girl's sake. I haven't spoken to either since.

One thing still bothered me. I couldn't understand how the spirits that were harassing that girl came through an email. How did they know anything about me, my husband, or the argument we had had? How had they even come out through an email?

I reached out to the only person I know who could possibly help: Mark Fults, my psychic medium friend. After he calmed me down, he explained it was all a clever "trick" spirits can use to "get inside your head" without really being there. Mark continued by telling me spirits and energies can read a person's aura picking up any information within 48 hours of what was said or done. He says it can take three or four days for the imprints to leave the recorded energy fields of the aura entirely.

Mark told me to be safe, I should always clear my aura before working with the paranormal. This can be done by meditation, prayer, cleansing, and grounding. He sent me a simple countdown meditation to reset my aura and told me to cut ties with the girl and her family which I had already done. I had never thought of grounding myself before analyzing audio, but I'm much more careful in all circumstances of a paranormal investigation now.

REDHEADED GHOST

A friend of mine and former EVP teammate, Melinda, had told me months before that strange things were happening in her home frequently and wanted me to see what I thought was going on; but no specific plans were made because she wanted to have the house to herself to remain somewhat secretive. She messaged me one night and asked if I had time to chat; I did. She sent a few texts saying her family was being increasingly affected and wanted my opinion asking if I could visit that night. I could, so I grabbed my equipment case, loading batteries and making sure my recorder and camera were charged, then hurried out the door for the short commute.

She came outside as soon as my car pulled into the drive; she had been watching for my arrival. I was greeted by a tense and unsure smile and knew the evening should be entertaining. She opened the door for me to enter and once inside, I set my equipment down and unpacked what I needed, immediately starting the digital recorder strapped on my arm. She began showing me through her home as I took photos, recounting different disturbances including noises as well as sightings of a shadow person. Melinda remembered lying down in bed one night and having the strange sensation of feeling someone or something get up off the mattress; she was alone.

She also felt watched and reported many times things had been moved or the family had heard noises at whatever end of the house they were not in at the time. Melinda admitted using a digital dousing device in her home; the same model she has is implemented by many paranormal investigators to obtain communication supposedly from the spirit world. She retrieved it powering it on while we were talking. One word that came through in the bedroom was 'Pat.' Melinda remembered that name belonged to the grandmother of a recent residential investigation. She felt the woman of the residence had related her own husband's temper to that of Melinda's spouse, Carl. Perhaps she had followed one member of the couple to their home.

Once done snapping pictures, we sat in the den, and she told me more details. Her family had been affected in different ways; while living in the home, they had suffered altered emotions and health problems including sudden illnesses, depression and severe anger. She told me many different accounts including the time Carl, becoming very angry, threw a chair after she had turned her back on him during an argument. She reported starting to turn around again, but her husband was already right behind her - his movements appearing much faster than normal which had been very unsettling.

I sensed eyes watching me but had no real fear of danger or ill intent directed at me as I moved from room to room, just a blanket creepiness. While we were talking, I caught movement: on the darkened surface of the flat screen TV, directly in front of me, I watched a beautiful woman with long red hair and a flowing white evening gown drift behind my chair. There was a white scarf around her neck that hung over the shoulders and continued down her back. She was one of the most beautiful women I'd ever seen. I turned to watch her pass behind me, but she was gone – disappeared instantly. Melinda asked, "did you see something?" I nodded smiling simply saying "who's the redhead?" Shocked that I had actually seen someone she replied "that's Carl's mother. We have some of her furniture here. She was very particular and liked her things to be *just so.* I simply said, "well, she's beautiful."

We talked a while longer, discussing her family's issues with the disturbances but we opted not to smudge her home so that she could watch it for a few days to see if my visit had stirred anything up. We also wanted to know if me acknowledging Carl's mother would help, or if she had even been a problem. Upon audio analysis the first message I got pertained to me: "she's seen others" and in reverse "she knows." The second one occurred while we were talking about the beautiful redhead and Melinda told me they had some of her furniture, the message said: "yeah, I don't want anything moved." In summation, I believe the first evp was the shadow person causing most of the negative disturbances; however, the beautiful redhead will never be a problem, unless something happens to her furniture.

TIME WARP

One night at a public guided tour of the old hospital, I had divided my team to make sure we all had information to tell the groups and could cover all three floors. We spent about 45 minutes to an hour per level, and I had finished the first-floor walk-through including an interactive investigation in the ER and the maternity ward. I'd walked back to the team room (Com Center), to get my equipment ready for the next group while the current group was taken to the third and then the second floor.

Sean burst into the room freaked out – which is extremely rare because, as co-founder of Elk Valley Paranormal, he was brought into ghost hunting as a skeptic of all things paranormal. Sean does a tremendous job debunking as much as he can during our investigations and tours. He is levelheaded, smart and entirely down to earth, and always easy-going and good-natured - except for tonight. Sean rushed to my side whispering almost incoherently, "I have to go!" But he couldn't go! We had 30 people participating in the public hunt this evening, and I needed him to stay focused on his favorite floor, second. Now he wanted to leave. Upset and not understanding what was so urgent, I said "you can't go! We've got all these people here tonight. I need you to cover two..." But he was out the door before I could stop him.

Confused and angry, I turned to hear Yoda and Matthew come in with the group of 10 ticketholders. Their eyes were wide, and each one was shaking his head as they walked straight to me and began to speak about something bizarre: somehow, they had started into the second-floor hall, but something had gotten them turned around, and they had become completely disoriented and somehow lost time. Following are the individual accounts of the evening.

Yoda
Lawrence "Yoda" remembered going up the stairwell at the end of the second floor farthest away from the east wing that holds ICU. This stairwell was the closest one to Com Center. He reported they walked out into the hallway with Sean leading the group and Matthew and Yoda were bringing up the rear to keep the tour group together. He remembered thinking to himself that it was going to take a little while to get all the way down to the double doors of the ICU. He said he and Matthew were talking to each other about it taking too long to get to the nurses' station. That first nurses' desk is only about a quarter of the way down the hallway, but to them, it was taking "forever and ever" to get there. Yoda continued "before we knew it, we had caught up to Sean all the way at the other end of the floor in the ICU." He says they spoke to Sean about it and he told them he had felt something weird too, but they weren't sure if he meant the timing or something else. Yoda finished by saying that Sean

remarked the hallway itself was strange that night, and they had thought so too.

Matthew

Matthew recalled they were guiding a tour of the old hospital and had gone to the third floor with the group. They then had walked down to the end of the children's side which is the western wing of the third floor and entered that stairwell to go down to second. He said they entered two from the central stairway (the west stairs and the middle ones are an entire wing apart). He explained that whatever stairwell they came out of seemed like the wrong one and was not where they should have ended up, but he brushed it off and kept the group moving along. Matthew said they walked down the hall "for what seemed like an eternity" and reached the opposite end of the hall where ICU is. The odd thing he reported was that they never got to the nurses' station which our team uses as a staging area on the second floor; a well-known landmark located where the hallway widens up that we know well enough to find with our eyes closed. Matthew says Yoda asked him "where did it go?" speaking about the nurses' area, saying he never saw it either. When they had a chance, they asked Sean about it, but Sean told them he had missed it too. In the wings of the hospital, the hallways are the normal width, but at the nurses' stations and in front of the elevators and the OR hallway, the area becomes much wider. Matthew finished by telling me the hall never opened up wider staying the same width from one end to the other.

Sean

Sean remembered breaking into groups, taking Yoda and Matthew with him. He said when they went to the second floor they used the stairs at the western end of the hospital, nearest the Com Center, as usual. Once on the floor, Sean says he asked everyone to go "lights out" by turning off all flashlights, and then waited a few minutes for everyone's eyes to adjust to the darkness. Sean says they started down the hallway and he had planned on taking the group down toward the OR to see the "death lights" then after that on to the ICU. He reports it seemed to be taking longer than normal, but he kept walking and guiding the group eastward. As he was looking straight ahead, Sean saw what he thought was a little boy, but he knew it wasn't possible. He decided not to say anything to anyone but kept watching the boy squinching up his eyes to see him better. He says he saw the boy sitting in front of the door straight ahead and somehow got turned around walking toward him. Sean reports becoming so disoriented that he thought they were on the west side of the hospital where they'd entered the second floor, but they weren't. Saying simply "I was completely turned around. We got to the nurses' station, and I thought that was the middle." He remembers skimming against the left side of the wall at the nurses' station thinking in a short while they would be by the elevators then could turn down toward the ORs. He says he remembers wondering "who moved the desk over closer to the wall?" making it so narrow at that section. He told the group "We're going a little farther." He said when they reached the last room of the hallway he even opened the door of the end room to check for the little boy, but there was no one there. Sean remembers thinking as he was walking and staring at the little boy that he was leading the group heading the opposite way. Sean finished by saying "somehow, we were at the ICU nurses' station, and I never remember passing the first nurses' station on the west wing, the elevators, or the hallway to the OR. Somehow, we lost time and our bearings. I'll never forget it."

***

What's interesting to me, is how something on the second floor caused all three experienced EVP investigators to be disoriented at the same time, but gave them each separate focuses. Sean was preoccupied with the little boy that wasn't there; Matthew concentrated on the stairs and the fact the hallway never widened; Yoda zeroed in on the much longer time it was taking to get to their destination. All three never remember passing the western nurses' station, the elevators, or the hallway to the ORs.

The Old Hospital is a strange, strange place, but on this particular night, three members of the EVP team experienced a time warp that involved utterly missing well-known building landmarks and entire areas with which we're very familiar. Sean, Matthew, and Yoda say that they will never forget that extraordinary experience.

Illustration inspired by *Intruder*

INTRUDER

My friends Justine and Donatien, live in a quiet cul-de-sac near the back of a subdivision in the county. Their property is peaceful and inviting; the home comfortable and filled with an eclectic mix of antiques, contemporary furniture, one-of-a-kind pieces "Don" has constructed, and their collectibles.

Justine told me that right after we performed a residential smudging ritual, she started noticing things had been moved in her home: candles leaning precariously in their holders, knives changing positions from their placement and other pieces out of place. She didn't discuss it with Don because he doesn't want to have any spirits in his home. Even though he deems himself a skeptic, he doesn't want there to be a chance of any paranormal disturbance.

In the nightstand, Justine keeps her gun next to her for protection. One night lying in bed while Don slept, she was watching television. The glow from the screen cast a bluish tint into the room and out into the hallway. She could see her dog, Lily, sleeping peacefully on the floor next to her side of the bed.

While relaxing, it was then out of the corner of her eye, Justine saw something move. She turned to look; a dark six-foot tall stranger was walking down the hallway. It looked like a person with a defined body and had a very distinctive gait. Lily heard the man, and immediately Justine grabbed her gun to protect herself and her family from the intruder, but no one was there.

She asked me to come over to see what I thought about the situation. I threw my things in the car and drove to her house. Evidently, Justine's uninvited guest knew she had asked for my help. Once parked, I pulled the equipment from the back seat of my car as Justine walked out to help me carry things across her lawn. As we reached the sidewalk pavers, I lost my balance falling hard on my left ankle. It happened before I could catch myself, and surprised both of us. It took me a few minutes for the throbbing to die down enough to walk inside, and by the time we got to her den, my ankle was very swollen.

We talked for a while as I stretched my injured ankle, then when I was ready, she showed me through her home. The house has a lovely big front porch with the den just inside the front door, and one can see straight through to the kitchen. There's a hallway to the right of the kitchen that leads to two bedrooms on the right, a bathroom and the master suite on the left. Through the kitchen and dining room area are doors to the backyard, laundry room, and garage.

During the walkthrough, the only creepy sensation I felt came from the antique mirror in Justine's spare bedroom which is on the opposite side of the hall from her master suite. We decided to perform a smudging ritual to push out the uninvited spirit.

Starting in the garage, the family's usual point of entry, I began chanting the words for the ritual as Justine walked ahead of me opening all the doors. We went clockwise through her home and afterward back outside, I saged Justine and had her sage me. Walking back inside, we found the house was noticeably lighter. After visiting a while longer, I left for home.

When Don arrived home, he, of course, could smell the sage, so Justine told him about cleansing their home, and he was appreciative. After the ritual, they've had no further disturbances or sightings.

I did find out the possible reason I felt uncomfortable around the antique mirror in the spare room; Justine's Ouija board was sitting above it, and she had recently used it on her last trip to South Carolina where something strange had happened to her group. A friend, Samantha, who is a medium had asked to borrow the board sometime after the South Carolina trip and before I performed the smudging ritual. Samantha told Justine when she picked it up, the board had growled at her.

PROBLEMS AT HOME

A family I know first lived in a subdivision in a house where the owner died. They began experiencing strange disturbances. One day outside, Amy watched as some unseen force pushed her four-year-old daughter Riley from one side then the other and down to the ground. Later Amy was reading inside and heard Riley calling "Mama!" She answered, "what Baby?" But turning to look no one was there. All five of the residents (Amy and her husband Chuck, children Riley and Lloyd, and Amy's mother Georgia Ann) fell down a particular set of stairs in the split-level level home at different times for no apparent reason. They videoed the cat eerily tracking something they could not see reporting there were no bugs inside or other pests.

In 2015, they were going to move in at Georgia Ann's in-laws' home and began renovations beforehand. Chuck would work putting up walls, painting or other things. One afternoon while working on the plumbing, he turned to see the head and shoulders of a dark figure in the hallway. Shouting "Hey! Hello!" He went after the intruder and found no one, but the chandelier in the hallway was swinging by itself. Merely walking through the hallway was not enough to make the light fixture move; it was moving by itself. He called his mother in law to report what had just happened and said the hair was standing up on the back of his neck while he was inside the house. Once he walked outside, he felt better. Walking back in he said into the empty home "okay, I'll finish later." He went to get the dog and came back to work more. There was a large board of sheetrock leaning solidly against one wall and as he walked by it lifted off the wall falling onto the opposite wall barely missing him. He called Amy to say "we've got a f**king problem. Call your ghost hunting friends."

Before EVP scheduled the investigation, a friend of the family, Doug Michaels came by for a visit and saw Chuck in a long black coat walking around the garage. Doug shouted at him, but Chuck kept walking as if he didn't hear them; so, he followed him calling again yelling his name. Doug went in the same direction around the garage to the open field, but there was no one. Freaked out, Doug got in his car and left calling Georgia Ann to tell her what it just happened. No one could explain it.

The family moved into the house in November 2015. Georgia Ann heard a loud knock at the door, but when she went to answer it, there was no one there. Shortly after that Georgia Ann broke her arm and separated her shoulder in a fall. She said it felt like someone "wrapped me up and tackled me" in the hallway.

One night Amy was standing in the kitchen and saw her son Lloyd creeping toward the bathroom grinning as he grabbed the doorknob opening it quickly while saying "what are you doing!?" He had been trying to scare someone; instead, he looked at his mother with a confused expression and asked: "did somebody just go in there?" She replied "no" which freaked him out a little. Even though Lloyd was also a skeptic, he occasionally said it felt like something was "on" him, and he'd have to go outside and say, "get off me!"

During Christmas, the family had a motion activated decoration they set on the back of the toilet that would talk to the person in the bathroom at the time. Riley would try to sneak into the room, but the animated piece would always start talking before she got inside scaring her. Every time she tried tiptoeing toward the bath, the festive piece came to life making her practically dive into her bedroom to get away from it.

In Georgia Ann's room, there is a door to her bathroom and a nook where she keeps her computer; she and the rest of the family have all had several weird things happen to the computers and other electronics in the house. In March 2016 Georgia Ann fell in her shower landing straddled over the side of the tub breaking several ribs. Although she wasn't dizzy and did not slip, she cannot say for sure that she was pushed. That summer, Amy was grilling outside and heard Georgia Ann fall hard inside the house. She was coming in the back door from the garage when she fell and broke her wrist but again cannot be sure if she was pushed or not.

The house sits on a strange plot with the driveway leading to a large garage that is sectioned off the front from the back with two entryways - one for the front and another for the back. There are two barns to the left of the garage one farther back than the other, and the house sits diagonally to the left front of the garage. A creek runs along the back of the land, and in the right corner, there is a tree growing. Amy says that is her least favorite area on the entire property; she even hates mowing back there.

One day while burying a beloved family pet, Lloyd's dog, he requested JJ be buried under the tree, about which Amy was not too excited. While they buried the pet, an owl flew to the tree just above their heads watching them. Soon after, Amy was driving and saw another owl. According to symbolism, an owl can be an announcer of death. Amy stopped the car to take a photo and told the owl speaking aloud saying "yes, we know JJ's gone you don't have to let us know anymore."

THE HOLIDAY RUSH

I had been 'rushed' before, you know, like when someone startles you by running up behind you or something, except in the paranormal world, being rushed by a ghost isn't so funny. As I said, I had been rushed by a spirit before, so I knew what that was like, but it had been in an old, very haunted building I used to go with my ghost hunting team to try out new equipment, or experiment with a technique we'd never before used. This time was different.

My husband had brought me to the mountains for my birthday, and an early Christmas getaway. We had booked a little cabin decorated throughout with black bears situated in a wooded area up the hill from a gently flowing stream.

When we arrived, the address was displayed by the statue of a carved black bear announcing the entry of the private drive. We both smiled when we saw it, and couldn't wait to get inside to unpack.

The cabin was the next to last house on the left before the cul-de-sac ended, and pulling into the parking area, you could see enough of a hillside to know there was a steep embankment there. Getting out of the truck, we both headed around the front of the vehicle to look over the hill. We saw a long staircase that led all the way down to just above the water's bank. The area was gorgeous and very peaceful.

We went inside and stepped into the entryway with a side table a few feet in front of us situated next to the couch. To the right of the front door was a long hallway with rooms leading off of it. As we unloaded the truck, we brought in luggage that went straight to the master suite on the left of the living area and took our toiletries into the bathroom. Groceries and games went to the long bar and the dining table that separated the kitchen area from the living room. Once unpacked, we set out to explore the rest of the cabin. The back door led onto a covered porch with rocking chairs and a hot tub. The view was spectacular. From inside the cabin, the high windows offered unrestricted views of the beautifully wooded hillside. Heading down the hallway, we could look straight into the open doorway of a second bath and saw there was another bedroom to the left of it. Also, on the left, halfway down the hall was a steep staircase leading down to the game room where we planned to spend hours playing pool with the billiard sticks with which my Dad had taught me how to play, each in its own special case. It was a large area separated by the stairway; on the right were two sets of bunk beds and a desk next to them, and to the left was a media room filled with movies, a snack area with a wet bar. The billiard table was the centerpiece of the big open room, and three doors led off it: one to the laundry room, another to a third bathroom, and the last door opened to the covered patio area and the backyard. There was a charcoal grill along with a picnic table and plenty of chairs to enjoy a cookout.

We decided to head into town for the afternoon and see the sights before relaxing at the cabin for the night. We noted three different putt-putt courses and knew we'd be competing against each other over the next few days. The town, dressed for the holidays, had a giant decorated tree in the center of its outdoor plaza surrounded by lighted reindeer and snowflakes. There were smaller trees in every shop, and cheerful wreathes on most every door and light post. Everyone was smiling. We grabbed a quick meal and visited a couple of stores before heading back toward the cabin.

Once back inside our home for the week, we grabbed drinks and my Dad's billiard sticks and headed downstairs. With music playing in the background, we laughed and took turns winning several games. Afterward, we sat in the hot tub for a few minutes and then went inside to shower off before bed. Warm, full and tired it wasn't hard to fall asleep.

Sometime after midnight I awoke and needed to use the bathroom but decided not to go into the closet one in our master suite to prevent disturbing my husband. As quietly as I could, I got up, went around the bed and walked out into the living room heading toward the hall in a faint light we had left on coming from the kitchen. The hallway itself was dark and somehow seemed longer now than it had earlier in the day. Passing the stairway opening I was startled by a sudden strange change in the air on the left side of my body from just below my shoulder up to my face - a silent scream so intense and palpable every hair stood up on the back of my neck. Something with the most incredible invisible force I had ever experienced, pushed me with a piercing screech I could not and did not want to hear. The rush of pressure was unmistakable in its hatred, and although I was terrified, I made myself remain calm walking the same speed down the hallway that had seemed to grow even longer and darker. When I reached the bathroom doorway, I flipped the light on as I walked inside and shut the door quickly without looking back toward the stairway. Immediately I felt a dread I couldn't shake. I knew when I finally opened the door once again, that I would come face to face with something or someone so horrible I would never be the same. Whatever it was wanted me out; it intended to make us leave.

I fought the panic that rose up inside me, washed my hands and took a slow deep breath. I stood holding the doorknob for several seconds willing myself to open the door and go back to my husband on the other side of the cabin where he slept, peacefully unaware of any danger. A quick, silent prayer thrown up for protection, I turned the knob deliberately and quickly throwing open the door to whatever horror awaited me. The hallway was empty. The air pressure had dropped, but it was not yet back to normal. There was static that I could still feel, but to a much less intenseness.

I walked quickly passed the stairs and could feel eyes watching, glaring. I forced myself to remain calm. If I could manage, this threatening was not going to be allowed to happen again and ruin our vacation. I needed sage, and I would find some when we went into town the next day. Of course, I would have to tell my husband about what had happened, but I doubted he would believe me. He usually listened without commenting, but I could see his thoughts by his expression.

A few hours later, after we both had gotten up, dressed and prepared to go into town, I told my husband about the intruder the night before. As I feared, I saw doubt in his eyes even though he agreed to help me find the incense I needed to smudge the cabin, but he never said a word. It took a while to find sage in this red and green painted mountain village, but we were directed to the one metaphysical shop in the region with only a few minutes until closing time. Rushing across the town, we made it with only 10 minutes to spare. The incense was straight inside the glass door, but all sage and other cleansing and blessing related items were sold out. Thinking I might have to resort to cedar or pine, I turned slightly to my left and saw bundles of herbs. I held my breath. There, among several filled baskets of products, laid one basket in the middle with only one piece in it - a single bundle of white sage. I picked it up, smelling it and smiled. Thank goodness there was one, but how odd there was only one. Coincidence? I don't believe in them. I needed sage and had found the last bundle inside the only metaphysical store in the area just before the shop closed for the weekend.

We drove back to the cabin while I explained to my husband what I needed him to do during the ritual to help me clear the space - stay ahead of me opening every door and drawer that could be a hiding place of darkness. He agreed to help me without question, probably just to humor me, but he agreed nonetheless.

I lit the smudge stick inside the front door, and my husband began opening everything in front of me so that the smoke from the sage could be wafted into every crevice. I started a continuous chant with the words my friend Mark Fults, psychic medium, had given me: "spirits of ill will, ill intent, cannot, will not cross this line." We moved clockwise from the door into the master suite and back around the living area into the dining area. Then we continued from the kitchen back through the front room and down the hallway into the stairwell; it was there the resistance grew increasingly stronger, and the air was thicker somehow than it had been. We pressed on clockwise through the downstairs from the sitting area into the laundry room and bath, then on to the other side of the stairs where there were bunk beds. That's where the feeling of anger was the strongest - the western corner of the cabin, so I made sure to concentrate there. We finished the basement and continued back upstairs turning left at the top of the steps. We went into the other bedroom then the bath in which I had been frightened the night before. Moving back down the hallway retracing our steps to the front door, we then walked outside. I smudged my husband in the fresh mountain air and then directed him to do the same for me, chanting the entire time. Once finished with the cleansing, we walked back inside; the air was noticeably lighter - even my husband noticed that.

We were able to continue our deserved vacation without incident, and I had no further interferences from the entity that had wanted us to leave. It's impressive how sage can lighten the dark mood of a place, and I'm so relieved it can. Happily, I can report I've not had to perform the smudging ritual in any other location for myself and my family, but to this day, I prefer to travel with a bundle of sage 'just in case.'

STRANGER AND STRANGER

In November 2015, I received an email from the founder of a paranormal team near the Virginia state line in East Tennessee. A truck driver, Michael, near our area (Middle Tennessee and Northern Alabama) had contacted Micki in need of help with some unusual problems. Because Micki's team was over three hours away, she asked if we could reach out to her client and offer our services. We were available, so Micki sent more information to me.

It seems Michael was at a hotel and called her early waking her up; it was 3:30 his time, but 4:30 AM for Micki. She recalled he was distraught. The young man told her he had moved into his house with a roommate about a month ago and upon settling in strange things began to happen. He reported sulfur smells and loud bangs. He also told her he heard footsteps that sounded like heavy men's boots walking back and forth in the hallway.

Michael said these things bothered him, but he tried to ignore them hoping they'd go away.

He told Micki that his roommate, Shannon had a Ouija Board and had used it quite often for at least three years. The last time Shannon used the board was while Michael was there which is when he reported the disturbances got worse: the bangs were louder, odors were more intense, and shadow figures began to appear.

The night before Michael called the East Tennessee team, he had taken his girlfriend out on a date, but upon their return, the house was in shambles, looking like it had been through a tornado. He said it appeared to have been ransacked: furniture and rugs were moved, dishes had been thrown from the kitchen cupboards onto the floor, sheets were ripped off the beds and shredded.

Michael's girlfriend, Alicia, had a closed, zippered bag that had been opened and all its contents were strewn about the house. Items from each of the bedrooms were found in other parts of the home completely destroyed.

The young man told Micki their pet dogs would growl and bark at "thin air" and had come running out of the bedrooms before like they were being chased by something. He said the animals were terrified and upon return from the date, the two dogs were sitting together on the couch whining amidst the chaos.

Michael decided to stay at a hotel for the night rather than risk any harm from whatever was in the house. He told the team founder he had taken photographs of the condition of the house before he left for the night. He also admitted using a couple of applications on his phone: one, a recorder that picked up an evp of something he couldn't decipher, and another that was a thermal imaging app which caught a face.

I reached out to Michael telling him we would be happy to help with the disturbances and tried to schedule a walk-through at his property with a few of my teammates. Scheduling ended up being most of the problem for us: of course, it was right in between Thanksgiving and Christmas which is always a busy time of year. In addition to the holidays, his truck driving calendar was very erratic, and to top it off, we'd had terrible weather including torrential downpours, flooding, and tornadic activity.

What struck me most was how Michael's stories continued to evolve - parts he'd forgotten to tell us the last time he'd spoken to one of my teammates or me or new occurrences. The drama was incredible. The latest phone call had unearthed the news that the roommate uses her Ouija Board to speak to "a nice demon" as she referred to it. The demon she said she was conversing with is the same demon that has come through many talking boards in the past and caused much destruction and many accidents. I don't repeat the name - ever, and neither does any person on my team.

While I was on the phone with Michael, I instructed him how to bind and bury the board and planchette which I hope he did. I also told him he needed to explain the danger of the demonic entity to the roommate and demand she never uses another board on his property. I highly doubt she will listen though.

On Tuesday night December 22, 2015, three members of my team and I, including Matthew were on a quick, fun ghost hunt at the Old Fayetteville (Lincoln County) Hospital. From experience, I knew the old building got very active around the Christmas holidays, and activity that night was indeed higher than normal, but in more unusual places than before. Then it got weird. We were in an old charting room in the maternity section of the hospital, and "Mary" was being quite talkative. Matthew heard her speak directly to him, and it was caught on a burst recording as well.

We were still doing short burst sessions when I got another phone call from a frantic Michael. One of the recorders was still going so the entire conversation was recorded. I explained to Michael that he was on speaker, so we could all hear, and several times during the phone call, strange whispers came from the phone. I asked the truck driver if his roommate or anyone else was sitting next to him, but he said Shannon was lying down in her room and his girlfriend was not there.

The spirit at Michael's house was reaching out to my team over the phone and dared us to visit. We even heard it say "chicken," but we're not sure if it was calling someone on my team that, or Michael. What's even more astounding is what the four of us heard on playback. Not only was the entity at Michael's home talking, but there was also another being in the room with my team speaking to Michael and the other spirit on the phone. It was a fascinating conversation to listen to, but Michael never heard the spirit voices, only me and my teammates.

We finished our burst sessions and then went back to our staging area, or what we call "Comm Center." Matthew and I talked about Michael and the spirit at his house, trying to figure out the best way to deal with the problem. When we reviewed the playback of that first conversation, we realized the entity did not have good intentions for anyone involved. After pondering the situation, we decided that being sensitive to such things, Matthew would scout the location out before we did anything else.

After our hunt concluded, Matthew drove by Michael's residence to get "a feel" for the entity there. When he reached home, he called and told me he had driven by the property and had immediately felt a presence in the passenger seat next to him. He told me he had spoken very plainly and said: "You have got to go now!" Strangely, at the exact moment when the entity left his vehicle, a herd of deer by the road ran away from Matthew's car. He likened it to the Bible story when Jesus cast out Legion causing it to go into the pigs, and they ran off the cliff and drowned.

Here is where the story gets even weirder. That first entity had departed Matthew's car - he felt it leave and knew it was gone which was good. Unfortunately, there was a second entity still in Matthew's vehicle, and he had no intention of bringing that thing into his home so continued driving to buy some time. While driving, he told that second entity it too had to go and could not stay. As Matthew drove closer to a certain fenced-in field, he felt like there was an invisible fence going across the road. When he crossed that line, he could feel the second entity being pulled out of the car, rather forcefully.

When he was sure that the second entity was indeed gone, he drove home. The next day, he researched the name of Shannon's "nice demon" to see what he could find out about it. Matthew reported to me the entity that named itself to Michael and Shannon had been documented back to 1816. As if that wasn't enough, this entity does not work alone; it has a friend that shows up about two or three weeks into playing with a Ouija board. Matthew had unknowingly encountered this friend also.

After that night, Michael never again contacted me or anybody else on the EVP team. Matthew has reported to me that he has not felt either of the entities in his life and says he can go the rest of his days happily without hearing from them again.

Matthew had a closing thought: "Ouija boards are not toys. I don't understand them and have no desire to. The supernatural realm is not something to casually play with. There are things that go bump in the night. I don't recommend anybody play with those things; and to anyone that is, please discontinue and find somebody to help you get rid of it. Approach the unknown with caution."

CYN SHRADER HILL

Cyn Shrader Hill is a native of Fayetteville, Tennessee, home of the very haunted Old Fayetteville (Lincoln County) Hospital. She works closely with the Hospital's owner making EVP the Host Team for special events and investigations throughout the year.

Sensitive and empathic, she has known 'others' were around her since she was very young. She has also been 'rescued' a few times over the years from very dangerous incidents. Cyn has helped other paranormal teams, both in the US and abroad as well as law enforcement officers with evp (electronic voice phenomenon) analysis. Her desire to see and speak to those on the other side has sent her to many of the most famous and fascinating locations: Gettysburg, Alcatraz, Goliad Presidio La Bahia, Winchester Mystery House, Birdcage Theater, Tower of London, Heian Jinju Shrine and Rothenburg Dungeons among others.

As the Founder of Elk Valley Paranormal, she formed EVP adding people to the group that not only mesh with each other but also bring complementary characteristics and talents to the team. EVP's members continually strive to find new and improved ways to reach answers for the paranormal and are determined to find some reason for hauntings. Overall, Cyn likes to be able to offer a client some sense of relief from any unexplained happenings, whether paranormal or not, that they've experienced. EVP isn't afraid to reach out to or work with other teams and has had several successful co-investigations.

Cyn has a BBA in Marketing from Middle Tennessee State University as well as a Letter she earned as Ole Blue the mascot. She graduated Summa Cum Laude from Vol State with an AAS in Physical Therapy, she traveled the country working in all healthcare settings. Certified by several organizations she enjoys teaching group fitness classes, has served as an adjunct instructor for Motlow State Community College and owned her own studio teaching all forms of Dance. Cyn is a presenter for area businesses, organizations, and events and has contributed her time and efforts to many fundraisers for the American Heart Association, the American Cancer Society, the Alzheimer's Association, Susan G. Komen Breast Cancer Association, and the Muscular Dystrophy Association to name a few.

Cyn was honored to be chosen as Storyteller by the owners of Young's Vintage Antiques during the *Spirits With The Spirits* event presented by Fayetteville Main Street in 2017 and plans to speak again for the 2018 function telling true ghost stories and tales of strange happenings surrounding the business.

Cyn was privileged to have an investigation photo (spirit feeding off of a Ouija Board in Lynchburg, TN) printed in Teal L. Gray's book *Shades of Angels*, and later, Teal included Cyn's first four stories in the book *Scared Senseless*. Cyn is currently working on her next book: *They're Speaking Are You Listening: My Most Compelling EVPs To Date*.

Contact: cynshraderhillauthor@gmail.com

MARK E. FULTS

Mark graciously agreed to create the stunning art work for the cover as well as the four beautiful and haunting illustrations in Cyn's book *Whispers In The Dark: True Ghost Stories and Eerie Tales.*

Mark Fults is a well-known psychic native to Chattanooga TN, now living in Pensacola FL, and is the author of *Chattanooga Chills*. In partnership with Teal Gray Worldwide, they have created 'GrayFults Press' to publish their own books, which already include *Shades of Angels* and *Spirited Tales* as well as his own: *The Corpsewood Catchfly: A Witch's Tale* and the first book in his trilogy *The Darkest Corner: Necrophilia, Necromancy, and the Functioning of a Working Psychic*, all available on Amazon. Mark produced illustrations and included several stories in each of Teal's bestselling books, and has more new books of his own forthcoming: *The Psychic Wormstitch* - a psychic tell all book, the next books in his trilogy *The Darkest Corner* - tales of necrophilia and necromancy, and of course *Chattanooga Chills Scream Louder* and *Chattanooga Chills Tales from the Grave*. He has several YouTube shows *Shadows Paranormal* including *Secrets of the Read House* by Stormline Films. Mark is currently working on the song to accompany his upcoming children's book *The Wind is Calling My Name*.

Contact: fultschat@aol.com

CPSIA information can be obtained
at www.ICGtesting.com
Printed in the USA
LVHW091256040419
612981LV00001B/32/P